# Decolonizing the Classroom

# Decolonizing the Classroom

## Confronting White Supremacy in Teacher Education

Jessica S. Krim and Jennifer M. Hernandez

LEXINGTON BOOKS
*Lanham • Boulder • New York • London*

Published by Lexington Books
An imprint of The Rowman & Littlefield Publishing Group, Inc.
4501 Forbes Boulevard, Suite 200, Lanham, Maryland 20706
www.rowman.com

6 Tinworth Street, London SE11 5AL, United Kingdom

Copyright © 2021 The Rowman & Littlefield Publishing Group, Inc.

*All rights reserved.* No part of this book may be reproduced in any form or by any electronic or mechanical means, including information storage and retrieval systems, without written permission from the publisher, except by a reviewer who may quote passages in a review.

British Library Cataloguing in Publication Information Available

**Library of Congress Cataloging-in-Publication Data**

Names: Krim, Jessica S., 1974- author. | Hernandez, Jennifer M., 1974- author.
Title: Decolonizing the classroom : confronting white supremacy in teacher education / Jessica S. Krim and Jennifer M. Hernandez.
Description: Lanham, Maryland : Lexington Books, 2021. | Includes bibliographical references and index.
Identifiers: LCCN 2021018558 (print) | LCCN 2021018559 (ebook) | ISBN 9781793607669 (cloth) | ISBN 9781793607676 (epub) ISBN 9781793607683 (pbk)
Subjects: LCSH: Teachers, Training of—Social aspects—United States. | Discrimination in education—United States. | Critical race theory.
Classification: LCC LB1715 .K65 2021 (print) | LCC LB1715 (ebook) | DDC 370.71/1—dc23
LC record available at https://lccn.loc.gov/2021018558
LC ebook record available at https://lccn.loc.gov/2021018559

# Contents

List of Figures and Tables — vii

1  White Teachers/Brown Students — 1
2  The Role of Teacher Education — 19
3  A Classroom Study of a Well-Meaning Teacher Educator — 41
4  Critical Race Theory — 59
5  What Are the Steps to Interrupting the Cycle? — 71

Appendix I: Reading List for White Teachers of Brown Students — 81
Appendix II: Sample of Course Description for Teacher Educators — 83
Bibliography — 85
Index — 95
About the Authors — 97

# List of Figures and Tables

## FIGURES

| | | |
|---|---|---|
| Figure 1.1 | Projections of Racial Composition of Students in the Classroom (US Department of Education 2016) | 2 |
| Figure 1.2 | Data Table Projecting Racial Composition of Students in Today's Classrooms (US Census Bureau 2018) | 2 |
| Figure 1.3 | Hispanic Enrollment in Teacher Preparation Programs by State (US Department of Education 2015) | 4 |
| Figure 1.4 | Location of Hispanic Serving Institutions (Hispanic Association of Colleges and Universities [HACU] 2016–2017) | 4 |
| Figure 1.5 | Black Enrollment in Teacher Preparation Programs by State Where Program is Located (US Department of Education 2015) | 5 |
| Figure 1.6 | Map of the Historically Black Colleges and Universities in the United States (HBCU Library Alliance 2020) | 5 |
| Figure 1.7 | Class Photo of Author's Grandmother, a Career Educator Who Taught in a Two-Room Schoolhouse in Pennsylvania from 1940 to 1960 | 7 |
| Figure 2.1 | Adapted from Bell, Goodman, and Ouelett, 2016 | 33 |
| Figure 2.2 | SJE and MCE Combination of Pedagogical Approach | 34 |

## TABLES

| | | |
|---|---|---|
| Table 3.1 | Creating a Multicultural Environment Using Multicultural Methods and Materials: Statistical Analysis of the Creating a Multicultural Environment Using Multicultural Methods and Materials Subgroup, Cultural Diversity Awareness Inventory Instrument | 51 |
| Table 3.2 | General Cultural Awareness: Statistical Analysis of the General Cultural Awareness Subgroup, Cultural Diversity Awareness Inventory Instrument | 52 |
| Table 3.3 | The Culturally Diverse Family: Statistical Analysis of the Culturally Diverse Family Subgroup, Cultural Diversity Awareness Inventory Instrument | 53 |
| Table 3.4 | Cross-Cultural Communication: Statistical Analysis of the Cross-Cultural Communication Subgroup, Cultural Diversity Awareness Inventory Instrument | 53 |
| Table 3.5 | Assessment: Statistical Analysis of the Assessment Subgroup, Cultural Diversity Awareness Inventory Instrument | 55 |

*Chapter 1*

# White Teachers/Brown Students

## INTRODUCTORY STATISTICS (DEMOGRAPHICS AND ACHIEVEMENT SCORES ON NATIONAL ASSESSMENTS)

According to the US Department of Education's 2016 report "The state of Racial Diversity in the Educator Workforce," "Diversity is inherently valuable. We are stronger as a nation when people of varied backgrounds, experiences, and perspectives work and learn together; diversity and inclusion breed innovation" (1). This is good news, as data tell us that our country is on the precipice of a major racial demographic shift of becoming more diverse in a variety of demographic constructs. For example, by 2024, white students will be outnumbered by students of non-white races in the classroom (figure 1.1).

This racial demographic shift in the classroom is reflective of the non-Hispanic white population in the United States shrinking overall; beginning in 2030, net international migration is expected to overtake natural increase as the driver of population growth in the United States because of population aging (Vespa, Armstrong and Medina 2018, 2–3). The white-non-Hispanic group will shrink "due to falling birth rates and rising numbers of death over time," and the most recently established census group, 'two or more races' is "projected to be the fastest growing racial or ethnic group over the next several decades." By 2060, non-Hispanic whites will make up only 36.5 percent of the classroom population (figure 1.2).

This national shift is being driven by overall increases in individuals who identify as Hispanic, Asian, or two or more races. In addition, there will be an increase in the number of foreign-born citizens, the likes of which we have not seen since 1890, as the natural increase of Americans will be surpassed by the net international migration (Vespa, Armstrong and Medina 2018, 4).

2                                    Chapter 1

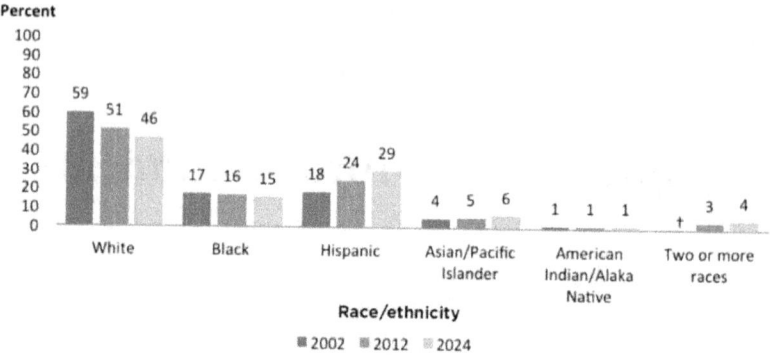

† Not applicable.

**NOTE:** Prior to 2008, separate data on students of two or more races were not collected. Detail may not sum to totals because of rounding. Data for 2024 are projected.

**Figure 1.1  Projections of Racial Composition of Students in the Classroom (US Department of Education 2016).**

Percentage of Children by Race and Ethnicity: Projections 2020 to 2060
By 2060, the share of children who are Two or More Races is projected to more than double.

| Characteristic | 2016 | 2020 | 2030 | 2060 |
|---|---|---|---|---|
| Total children under 18 (in thousands) | 73,642 | 73,967 | 75,652 | 80,137 |
| One race | | | | |
| White | 72.5 | 71.6 | 69.4 | 62.9 |
| Non-Hispanic White | 51.1 | 49.8 | 46.9 | 36.4 |
| Black or African American | 15.1 | 15.2 | 15.5 | 16.0 |
| American Indian and Alaska Native | 1.6 | 1.6 | 1.5 | 1.4 |
| Asian | 5.2 | 5.5 | 6.3 | 8.1 |
| Native Hawaiian and Other Pacific Islander | 0.3 | 0.3 | 0.3 | 0.3 |
| Two or More Races | 5.3 | 5.8 | 7.0 | 11.3 |
| Hispanic | 24.9 | 25.5 | 26.5 | 31.9 |

Note: The official population estimates for the United States are shown for 2016; the projections use the Vintage 2016 population estimate for July 1, 2016, as the base population for projecting from 2017 to 2060. Percentages will not add to 100 because Hispanics may be any race.

**Figure 1.2  Data Table Projecting Racial Composition of Students in Today's Classrooms (US Census Bureau 2018).**

National demographics show us that the composition of the United States looks very different today than it did in the last quarter-century. There are increases in the numbers of multi-generational and shared households, cohabitation among unmarried parents, marriage between individuals from different racial groups, and instances of motherhood among unmarried women. Worldwide, there are increases in both emigration and refugee populations, and "the number of births to Muslim women is projected to exceed births to Christian women by 2030-2035" (Cilluffo and Cohn 2017).

On the other hand, when we examine the demographics of K-12 teachers in public schools, we see that they are typically female, middle class, white, and monolingual (Howard 2006). In 1988, 87 percent of teachers in grades 1–12 were white, and in 2012, this figure dropped to 81 percent. Reported in July of 2016, US Department of Education Report: The State of Racial Diversity in the Educator Workforce Summary of Findings reported that the Elementary and Secondary teachers are homogeneously white reporting at 80 percent of the in-service teacher demographic. Principals are also overwhelmingly of the white race, at 80 percent in 2012 (US Department of Education 2016). Although the racial diversity among teachers and principals is decreasing, this is happening at an insufficient pace to match the increasing diversity of K-12 students; while our students are becoming more diverse at a rate of 8 percent, are teachers are only becoming more diverse at a rate of 4 percent, and principals at a rate of 3 percent.

In later chapters we will provide a detailed discussion about the price that our students, families, and communities pay for being part of a system that caters to the white race. For introductory purposes, however, we would like to preface this discussion with another—that of the impact that is experienced by K-12 children of color in the areas of achievement test scores, out-of-school suspensions, and dropout rates. In 2017, Black students in grade 4 scored, on average, 26 points lower than their white peers on reading achievement tests. Hispanic students scored an average of 23 points lower than white students. In grade 8, Black students scored an average of 19 points lower, while Hispanic students scored an average of 25 points lower than their white peers. In 2017, math achievement test scores demonstrated more damning results; Black students scored an average of 25 points lower than their white peers in 4th grade, 32 points lower than their white peers in 8th grade, and Hispanic students scored an average of 19 points lower in the 4th grade and an average of 24 points lower in the 8th grade, when compared to their white peers. This data represents a widening of the achievement gap from elementary school to middle school.

In 2013–2014, Black students were 13.7 percent more likely to receive out-of-school suspensions than peers of other races: This is twice as many as students of American Indian/Alaskan native descent (n = 6.7 percent), three times as likely as students of two or more races (n = 5.3 percent), three times as likely as students of the Hispanic/Pacific Islander race or ethnicity (n = 4.5 percent), five times as likely as students of the white race (n = 3.4 percent), and twelve times as likely as students of Asian descent (n = 1.1 percent) (NCES 2019). While the dropout rate between students of white and Black races is similar, students of Hispanic race or ethnicity hold a higher dropout rate overall (NCES 2019).

This disparate trend of racial inequity in teacher demographics is perpetuated at public institutions of higher education. Not only are the majority of the faculty (n = 80 percent) (NCES 2009) white, the majority of preservice teachers enrolled in teacher education programs are also white. However, the US Department of Education reports that in 2013–2014, in specific geographic areas, there were higher rates of preservice teachers of color in teacher preparation programs; Black and Hispanic preservice teachers are more likely to be enrolled in these programs in states on the eastern and southern coasts of the United States (USDE 2016).

As illustrated in figures 1.3 and 1.4, the location of high numbers of Hispanic enrollment in teacher preparation programs closely correlates with the location of Hispanic Serving Institutions (HSI). This trend is similar to

Figure 1.3   Hispanic Enrollment in Teacher Preparation Programs by State (US Department of Education 2015).

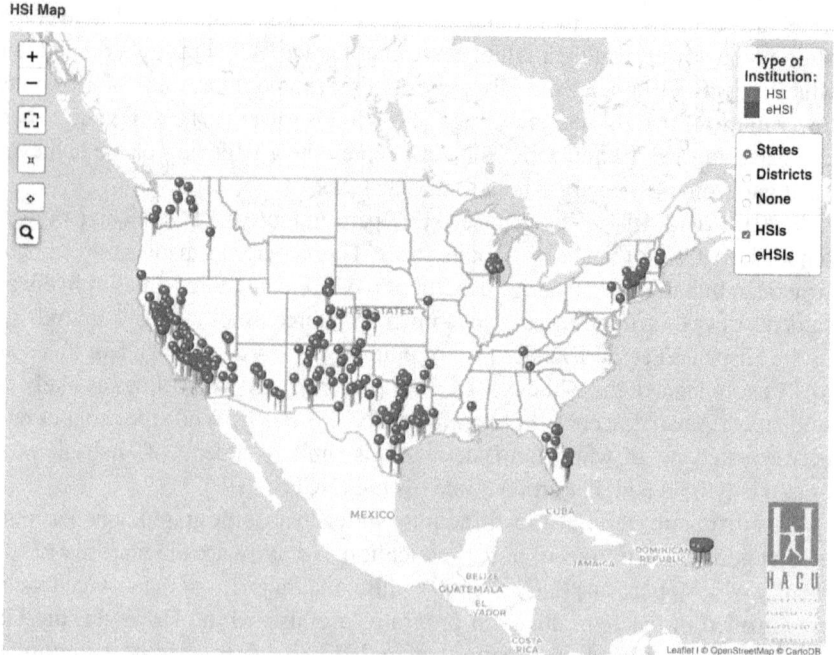

Figure 1.4   Location of Hispanic Serving Institutions (Hispanic Association of Colleges and Universities [HACU] 2016–2017).

Figure 1.5 Black Enrollment in Teacher Preparation Programs by State Where Program is Located (US Department of Education 2015).

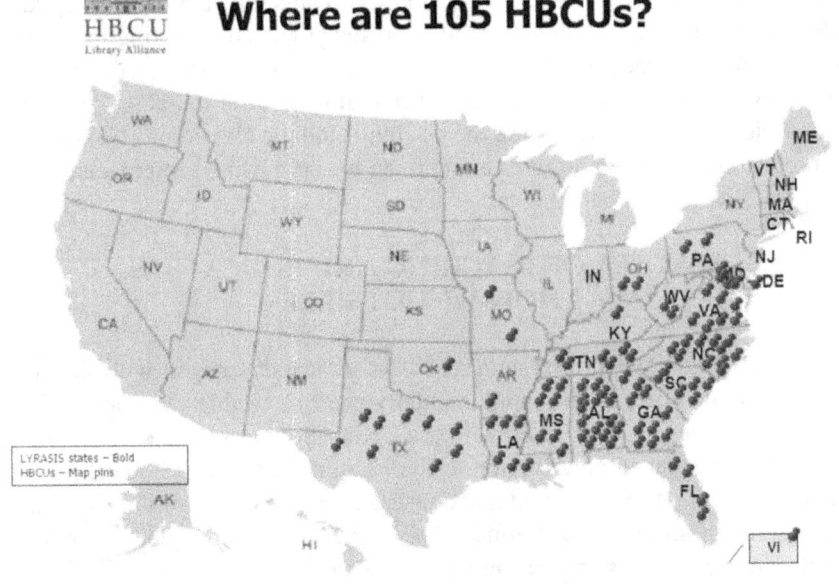

Figure 1.6 Map of the Historically Black Colleges and Universities in the United States (HBCU Library Alliance 2020).

that of Historically Black Colleges and Universities, as shown in figures 1.5 and 1.6.

There are higher rates of preservice teachers of color enrolled in teacher preparation programs in Historically Black Colleges and Universities than in non-HBCU schools, and preservice teachers of color are more likely to enroll in alternative-route certification programs than the traditional undergraduate programs. The close correlation between universities that serve Black and LatinX populations with the number of Black and LatinX preservice teachers enrolled in teacher preparation programs implies that these universities and areas will be leaders in the next five to twenty years, producing qualified educators that will be of demand nationwide. It follows that these teacher education programs are ones to watch as their approaches provide a much needed non-white perspective. At the same time, simply replicating the methodology that is used within these institutions is insufficient. Overall, when we look at post-secondary completion levels within all teacher preparation programs, 73 percent of white undergraduates complete within six years, compared with 49 percent of LatinX undergraduates and 45 percent of Black undergraduates (USDE 2016). This data points to a deeper, more systemic issue than simply co-opting a HBCU's approach to teacher preparation programs; if program demographics evidence that primarily white students are being served, it stands to reason that equity is not being addressed. There are no coincidences. Teacher preparation programs in Primarily White Institutions or Programs (PwIs) need to not only look at how often social justice is lacking from their curriculum, but they need to have an authentic and fearless conversation about why it is lacking from their curriculum—as it is the absence of this discussion from the curriculum, the teaching, and the classrooms that enables these institutions and programs to continue to serve white supremacist goals.

## HISTORY OF TEACHING AND EDUCATION: HOW WE GOT HERE

The US public education system as we know it today began with the "one room schoolhouse" model, predominantly used in established communities across the country. This German-based educational system evolved from Kant's philosophical contribution to the Enlightenment, and it set the foundational structure for curriculum and instructional practices still in use today. Demographic measures of public schools reflected a homogeneous population of white students and teachers (figure 1.7).

The "science" of Eugenics was a commonly accepted explanation for the widely held belief that only white people were entitled to education. For persons deemed not worthy of being educated, alternate educational opportunities were pieced together with few resources creating separate and unequal educational opportunities (Troen 2008). The Indian Removal Act of 1830 and the Indian Appropriations Act of 1851 resulted in the formation and establishment of common areas of land (reservations) where indigenous people were forced to live and could not leave. In 1860, the first Indian boarding school was established, and Native Americans were forced to

Figure 1.7 Class Photo of Author's Grandmother, a Career Educator Who Taught in a Two-Room Schoolhouse in Pennsylvania from 1940 to 1960.

send their children to these schools. Here, schools attempted to indoctrinate Native American children into European cultural norms through physical punishments, public humiliation, and conditioning (Zinn 1980), which included cutting their hair and forbidding them to speak their mother tongue.

Migrant workers and undocumented laborers from China and Latin American countries, and their families, have contributed to American society from its inception. They have been required to pay taxes to fund the education that their children were forbidden to access. Before child labor laws, children of migrant and undocumented laborers were expected to work next to their parents and family members. There was no expectation that they would ever be provided with the opportunity to attend the schools of their white peers (Zinn 1980). Women in institutions of public education were tracked (Burris and Garrity 2008) for domestic courses like cooking, sewing, etiquette, and other clerical tasks, designed to ensure their ability to work until they married. The core educational opportunities offered to women at this time were a direct reflection of socially constructed gender roles. The impact of such policies is still felt today as school districts, universities, and industry are having to bridge the gap for the disparity created by these outdated social norms by creating and providing incentives to recruit and retain women in the STEM disciplines (Breede et al. 2011).

In 1847, Missouri law prohibited the teaching of Black people to read or write. However, this law was not effective in the city of St. Louis. Black churches and a few white churches had held classes prior to the Civil War to educate Black people. Similar to the migrant workers and undocumented laborers from China and Latin American countries, citizens of the city of St. Louis were being required to pay taxes to fund the education that their children were forbidden to access. During and after the Civil War, private organizations began providing education for Black children. In 1865, state law was passed that allowed Black children to receive an education in a segregated space (Gersman 1972). The events in Missouri represent how most of the states in the nation addressed the education of students of color. There were instances of violent unrest and protests against segregation or lack of educational opportunities for Black children, but these instances were the exception rather than the rule for the majority of the nation. Since the First World War, only white students had access to public education funded through tax dollars; students of color were left to seek educational experiences offered through philanthropic generosity and churches. At times, educational resources, schooling locations, and teachers were pieced together from any available resources to educate children (Gersman 1972). These patterns of segregation continued for the next 100 years.

At the time of the writing of this book, Ruby Bridges celebrated her sixty-second birthday. Pictures of Ruby's bravery as a young girl in 1954, walking into the first integrated school in Louisiana after the passing of Brown v Board, fill civil rights museums and historic landmarks in Jim Crow South, a visual reminder that southern schools of this era were forced to desegregate. When put into perspective, the implementation of Brown versus Board occurred only fifty-three years ago. The documented right of Black children to attend publicly funded schools with their white peers is little over five decades old. This very brief summary of public education's history outlines the scaffolding of policy, practice, and curriculum resulting in an educational system that in its infancy never intended to include students of color. Despite these steps forward, there is still much to accomplish. Today's teacher preparation programs offer curriculum describing the history of public education in foundational courses but fail to address the racialized history of white dominance. Programs frequently access a white savior mentality by focusing on the contributions public education has made to poor and marginalized communities after Brown v Board, yet completely ignore representing the fact that students with disabilities were not granted access to publicly funded education until 1973.

An example of this white savior mentality, Bauer introduces in her analysis the concept of "benevolent Whiteness": this self-imposed trope of selfless service of white women in relation to Black and Brown folx through systemic schooling is the feminized extension of white supremacy. Whiteness encompasses a belief in individual heroism, including the dangerous notion that one white teacher can "save" individual or particular problem students. This "savior" narrative ignores the systemic inequity at the foundation of public education (Bauer 2020). The myth of teachers as heroes is encompassed in the settler colonial histories of white, female teachers. This narrative reduces the complex history of public education to individual narrative of salvation stories around white women magically impacting and teaching Black and Brown children in a way Black and Brown teachers could not. These narratives justify a belief in the inherent pathology of poor Black and Brown communities and reinforce the imaginary of the necessary "white women's burden to save these communities" (Bauer 2020).

## WHITE SUPREMACIST POLICY IN PUBLIC EDUCATION

The fact that the curriculum of public schools has had a Eurocentric focus and white-dominant perspective since Kant's contribution to the Enlightenment demonstrates that there is much work that needs to be done around curriculum. Linked to this history of education, public schools have been considered a predominantly white space. Curriculum was taught in a binary of winners and losers making Americans the winners, the innovators, and the holders of progress while ignoring the history of exclusion and oppression within its institutions. In times of America's questionable progress or muddied "wins," the language used to communicate historical events is altered to minimize the losses. For example, in 1953, the United States labeled the Korean War as a "conflict" after recognizing they were in an unwinnable situation, leaving the country without fulfilling its original goals of preventing North Korea from invading South Korea. We see the same for Vietnam; while US troops were on active duty, it was referred to as the Vietnam War on televisions across American homes. Once the US troops left Vietnam without resolution, after twenty years of fighting, history textbooks used in school curriculum began to label it as the "Vietnam Conflict."

Teacher preparation programs structure their instructional strategies and pedagogies to address marginalized students with labels such as "at-risk," "free and reduced lunch population," "below grade level," and "tiered targeted interventions." The power of this language allows teachers to remove the history of exclusion and oppression within public education and place blame on societal factors like poverty. Because public education has been integrated for only fifty-three years, the institution itself is still working to remedy the generations of impairment that has been bestowed upon students who have been historically excluded from high-quality educational experiences.

Within the white supremacist curriculum, these labels have two primary functions. First, they do not pay homage to the long history of segregation and oppression of students of color, allowing white people to avoid discussion of the role of white supremacy. Second, when discussing the inadequate educational outcomes for students of color, labels constructed by state and federal education agencies redirect blame to societal factors such as poverty. Using these labels supports the emotionality of Whiteness in its blaming of poverty for education deficits rather than white supremacy's role in institutional racism within the US public education system (Matias, Montoya and Nishi 2016). White faculty members who teach white teacher candidates about how to access specific instructional strategies in order to "deal with" the achievement gap for students of color, is an attempt to absolve faculty and teachers of white guilt; serving only to establish and promote the historical ideology of eugenics and entitlement of public education for white children without having to acknowledge feelings of racism or superiority to students of color.

White supremacy is blatantly misdirected in its approach to the behavior management of students within public education. After the horrific incident of Columbine High School in 1999, the merging of criminal justice and public education systems have resulted in the criminalization of student behavior (Casella 2003). Educational policy includes crime policy, child welfare policy, and other social policies intended for the youth that attend schools. The Zero Tolerance Policy (ZTP) that came about after the Columbine tragedy was developed with three national initiatives in mind. First, the development of violence prevention and conflict resolution programs in schools. Second, an attempt toward implementing gun control laws. Lastly and most importantly, this policy required implementation of punitive and judicial forms of discipline in schools as a prevention and consequence of crime. The Safe Schools Act of 1994 (PL 103-227) and the Safe and Drug-Free Schools and Communities Act of 1994 (PL 103-382) provided funding for prevention and mediation programs addressed in the first initiative. The second initiative was addressed with the Gun-Free School Zones Act of 1990 (PL 101-647). Punitive discipline and gun control were both addressed in the Gun-Free Schools Act (PL 103-227). This resulted in the expulsion of students who brought a gun to school. However, in order to force compliance by the school districts, the government amended the Elementary and Secondary Education Act of 1965 to withhold federal funding if a school did not conform to these initiatives. In 1995, amendments within these acts were made to replace "firearm" with "weapon," which allowed schools to use a broad category for any object that could be used as a weapon; including pocket knives, nail clippers, and nail files (Alexander and Alexander 2009).

## POLICE IN SCHOOLS

The concept of police officers in schools was first seen in the UK in 1951 and Canada in 1958. In the United States, the first high school to create a police-school liaison was in Flint, Michigan, in 1958. The global definition of the general functions of the police officer in the school setting included that of; counseling, substance abuse prevention, crime prevention, school safety improvement, creating trust and rapport with students, investigation, reporting and documenting incidents, and serving as a liaison between the schools and the criminal justice system. Currently, American police officers in schools are given the title School Resource Officers (SROs) and fulfill these roles while dually creating a police presence in schools through the acts of policing, surveillance, investigation of possible crimes, and handling disruptive students. SROs are dressed in uniform and fully armed with weapons, handcuffs, tasers, and mace. A study conducted in New York City Public Schools in 1996 concluded that a fortress-like security is toxic to school culture. Teachers complained of instructional disturbances during class due to interference noise in the hallways emitted from between the two-way radios that officers carry for communication, and principals complained of a perceived unclear order of authority. SROs do not report to school officials; instead, they report to state justice systems. Due to unclear boundaries of authority, in many areas, SROs have also taken over student discipline, creating a "jailhouse" feel to the school culture (Richard 2007).

The combination of school policies designed to reduce violence and the presence of police officers has had the effect of "criminalizing" a broad range of activities of misconduct that pose no real threat to safety. Behaviors once painted as disruptive and troublesome, including; cursing, disrespect, verbal threats of fighting with peers, verbal threats toward staff, non-compliance, and not completing assignments have now been handled formally by law enforcement in many areas. Police have enormous discretionary power in the handling of juveniles. Officers are expected to use their discretion in deciding whether to arrest a student or simply order them to stop (Richard 2007). The combination of these Zero Tolerance Policies, federal legislation, and an established police presence in schools has institutionalized the school-to-prison nexus. While it is clear that the goal of ZTP is to ensure the safety of the students and teachers, a harsh "one strike and you are out" policy conflicts with the fundamental principles of school law which hold that the discipline of a student must take into account the specific facts for each individual student. ZTP does away with the concept of "innocent until proven guilty" and sacrifices proportional responses to student behavior with mandated discipline (Richard 2007).

The American Bar Association passed a resolution opposing ZTP because it is shown to have a discriminatory effect and mandates either expulsion or referral of students to juvenile or criminal court without regard to the circumstances or nature of the offense or the student's history (ABA 2001). Moreover, ZTP derails the educational process by turning schools into holding facilities and filling them with law enforcement professionals. The effectiveness of ZTP is questionable because it alienates children, exacerbates misbehavior, and criminalizes behavior that was once handled by school administrators (Freis and DeMitchell 2007). In the aftermath of sensational school violence, legislators and school administrators adopted ZTPs that lead to the expulsion of a student for any infraction of rules barring weapons, drugs, alcohol, gang-like activities, and even speech (117 ALR 5th 459 2004). The application of ZTP to student behavior such as fist fighting and verbal abuse is clearly outside the scope of the original legislative intent (Brady, 2001).

The school-to-prison nexus has been created by a set of discipline policies and strategies of social control in schools that make it more likely that students will be "pushed" out of school and into a life reality that expedites delinquent and criminal behaviors and as a result, excluded from the known social and educational benefits associated with the educational system. Latina/o students are historically shown to be disproportionately punished at school, which creates negative impacts on their educational progress and inhibits success (Peguero, Bondy and Shekarhar 2017). Black, Hispanic, and American Indian students are more likely to experience exclusionary discipline than their white counterparts. That is to say, students of color get disproportionately punished and suspended (Ford 2016). The Civil Rights Data Collection found that in the 2013–2014 school year, Black K-12 students were 3.8 times as likely as white students to receive one or more out-of-school suspensions. Among all K-12 students, 6 percent received one or more out-of-school suspensions, but the percentage differed by race and gender: 18 percent for Black boys, 10 percent for Black girls, 5 percent for white boys, and 2 percent for white girls (Ford, 2016). Evidence shows us that white teachers demonstrate their socialized bias of Black boys, when they disproportionately discipline and surveil Black males for minor and subjective school disciplinary infractions (Bryan 2017). Through history and socialization, deficit messages, biases, and stereotypes about students of color are passed down from one generation to the next (e.g., from in-service teacher, to preservice teacher, to white 3rd grader). These microaggressions and biases that are revealed in the behavior of white teachers and their students impact their overall interactions with students of color. There must be an intentional focus for white teachers and their teacher education programs to interrupt such historical perceptions of students of color (Bryan 2017). There is an overwhelming white, middle-class, and female population in the teaching profession, and it is this population that remains fixed because most teacher education programs continue to serve white females as future educators of K-12 classrooms (Bryan 2017). If teacher education programs do not interrupt such historical perceptions of students of color, then white teacher candidates have the probability of entering and exiting teacher education programs with deficit beliefs and assumptions about students that do not look like them. In other words, these biases have implications beyond preservice teacher preparation (Bryan 2017).

## MULTICULTURAL EDUCATION RECONCEPTUALIZED

Attempts to address the disparity of the demographic profile of teachers and students in K-12 public school settings are typically addressed by educating teacher candidates about multicultural education, as a pedagogical approach: "Multicultural education refers to any form of education or teaching that incorporates the histories, texts, values, beliefs, and perspectives of people from different cultural backgrounds" (www.edglossory.org 3.6.2016). Reaching its peak in the 1980s, this approach has run its course through an era when protection of white emotionality was thought to be acceptable. Continuing to practice this approach as part of the white supremacist curriculum encourages teachers and students to practice "simulated tolerance" (Evans-Winters and Hoff 2011). Simulated tolerance is exhibited by behavior patterns that seem to follow a philosophy of "I believe *this*, but I teach *that*." This compartmentalization of behaviors is witnessed when teachers willingly go into high needs areas but once there, still harbor negative beliefs about the students and the community or teach by way of a deficit model (Ryan 2012; Waddell 2013). It is possible that teacher preparation programs support this simulated tolerance by encouraging teacher candidates to hide themselves from their students, by professing phrases such as; "there should be a 'teacher-self' and a 'personal self,'" or "don't share too much with your students," and "keep a professional boundary." While all these are true within the context of encouraging teacher candidates to create a professional rapport with students, within the white supremacist curriculum evident in teacher education programs, it is necessary to call attention to and distinguish the two the collapsed ideas of both encouraging teacher candidates to grow as professionals and emphasizing the importance of doing the "inside work" required to be an effective inclusive educator. According to Howard (2006), "We cannot fully and fruitfully engage in meaningful dialogue across the differences of race and culture without doing the work of personal transformation."

## A SENSE OF URGENCY AROUND GLOBAL DEMOGRAPHIC SHIFT

In 2002, the Partnership for 21st Century Learning began focusing on the implementation of the "21st Century Framework for Learning"; as a way to restructure or supplement curriculum in US schools, and prepare today's students for a career in tomorrow's global society. Learning and innovation skills within the framework include creativity, collaboration, communication, and critical thinking. Throughout the framework is a "global awareness" strand, challenging teachers to prepare students to "use 21st century skills to understand and address global issues; learn from and work collaboratively with individuals representing diverse cultures, religions, and lifestyles in a spirit of mutual respect and open dialogue in personal, work, and community contexts; and understand other nations and cultures, including the use of non-English languages" (Framework for 21st Century Learning definitions, p. 3). This strand influences learning and performance goals in areas of creativity and innovation, communication and collaboration, flexibility and adaptability, and social and cross-cultural skills, resulting in a variety of objectives: *"working creatively with others,"* teaching students to be open and responsive to new and diverse perspectives; *"communicate clearly,"* teaching students to demonstrate ability to work effectively and respectfully with diverse teams; *"adapt to change,"* teaching students to work effectively in a climate of ambiguity and changing priorities; *"be flexible,"* teaching students to understand, negotiate, and balance diverse views and beliefs to reach workable solutions, particularly in multicultural environments; *"interact effectively with others,"* teaching students to know when it is appropriate to listen and when to speak; and *"work effectively in diverse teams,"* teaching students to respect cultural differences and work effectively with people from a range of social and cultural backgrounds. These strands throughout this framework have the potential to provide an arena in which to address the white supremacist curriculum in place.

The 21st Century for Learning initiative is also an example of why today's students need to learn skills that will allow them to be competitive in a global market. It professes teaching knowledge, skills, and dispositions that promote diverse thinking, acceptance of other perspectives, communicating, and finding creative solutions to problems. As such, it follows that in order to do the transformational work of education, teachers involved in this, or any initiative, must do the "inside work," shrug off the lure of simulated tolerance, and model this practice for ourselves and our students. Teachers today must practice the honoring of diverse peoples, languages, perspectives, and to do this, they must first face the obstacles that maintain the status quo of white supremacist curriculum. It is the opinion of the authors that it is the role of teacher preparation programs to encourage teacher candidates to challenge themselves in doing this internal work. The Equity Group (Adams 2016) is an example of a collaborative effort in which this type of work has been conducted with teachers, illustrating that the challenges of such an effort must be met with participants who are willing to contribute their own authenticity, fallibility, and ability to champion for each other within the group. Creating such an environment within a teacher preparation program calls for a new paradigm within teacher education, the training of teacher educators, and the education system, itself.

Equally as vital as the shift from a white supremacist curricula to a socially just curricula, is the need for diversity in teaching faculty. Students need to both hear the voices of the marginalized and see representations of themselves in the classroom (context) and curriculum taught (content). Far too few teacher candidates report ever having a teacher or color in their K-12 experience. Because of public education being raised and maintained in a state of Whiteness, people of color or marginal status rarely see education as a viable career option. Additionally, because of the over-policing of students of color, a white-dominant curricula, and a lack of representation, university preservice teachers of color rarely enter teacher education programs. Their own public school experiences of the educational system being hostile, overtly racist, and genuinely emotionally and physically unsafe results in a lack of trust and desire to participate in the educational system by choice.

## THE CORRELATION BETWEEN PRESIDENTIAL ADMINISTRATION AND SCHOOL-BASED CONFLICT AND DISTURBANCE

Within our current social context, the overtly white supremacist rhetoric has created a larger division in our nation's democracy, and a haven within the rhetoric of our current administration in the White House, which refuses to acknowledge the humanity of asylum seekers, immigrants, and refugees. Unfortunately, we cannot look in this direction for the solution to the topic of this book. In 2016, a school in New Haven, Connecticut which prides itself on serving its high percentage of immigrants within a sanctuary city, reported that young white students were chanting "build the wall" while banging their fists on the tables in the cafeteria at lunch the day after the presidential election results were announced. In another school, 12 miles away in the non-sanctuary city, of Wallingford, Connecticut, students wore "MAGA" hats and chanted anti-immigrant rhetoric and anti-semitic slurs while in their cafeteria.

Our current elected leader has empowered white supremacy in his campaign speeches and continues to do so while holding office. Initiating claims that there are "good people" on both sides of the white supremacist rally in Charlottesville, VA, where a young lady protesting white nationalism lost her life and many people of color were injured, is a demonstration of this. His white nationalist rhetoric is exemplified when referring to Haiti and countries in Africa as "shithole" countries. The policy of family separation and caging young children, including infants, and imprisoning asylum seekers at the border has an enormous impact on young people and families. Unfortunately, teacher preparation programs have not done the work to prepare preservice teachers for this level of overt racism. Without doing their own personal work around inherent and implicit bias, and being willing to confront their behaviors on a daily basis, novice teachers will be ill-equipped to see the current events with a historical perspective, and this will impact how they address these events with their students. Because our schools reflect our communities, the role of the educator to take a balcony view of the power dynamics at play within schools and in our nation is crucial for the care and well-being of all students to feel as though they are an equal participant in their classrooms.

In a report released by the Southern Poverty Law Center, the Teaching Tolerance program, which is dedicated to the reduction of marginalization of marginalized students in public schools, noted that 40 percent of students heard derogatory language directed at students of color, Muslims, immigrants, gender nonconforming students, and students identifying as LGBTQAI+. Additionally, half of the students reported that they are targeting one another based on the candidate they supported during the election (SPLC 2016).

This survey asked educators, administrators, and students about the impact of the election and election rhetoric during the 2016 election, and over 2,500 educators described specific incidents of bigotry and harassment that can be directly traced to election rhetoric. These incidents include graffiti (including swastikas), assaults on students and teachers, property damage, fights and threats of violence. Because of the heightened emotion, half are hesitant to discuss the election in class. Some principals have told teachers to refrain from discussing or addressing the election in any way. Although two-thirds report that administrators have been "responsive," 40 percent don't think their schools have action plans to respond to incidents of hate and bias. Eighty percent of students surveyed report heightened anxiety on the part of marginalized students, including immigrants, Muslims, African Americans, and LGBT students. Ninety percent of educators who responded have seen a negative impact on students' mood and behavior following the election; most of them worry about the continuing impact for the remainder of the school year (SPLC 2016).

In the self-reporting survey of over 96,000 public schools, the overwhelming impacts on schools from this divisive rhetoric include the increased targeting and harassment of a student with marginalized identities and then exploded in a number of incidents after the election results. Broadly speaking, the survey results indicate that schools with significant numbers of Black and LatinX students and immigrant students of color are experiencing what many teachers named trauma and the symptoms of trauma in their responses. Finally, in diverse schools where there is no group in the majority, teachers report that students are tense, have lost trust in each other and are struggling to get along. The divisions opened by the election run deep in these schools (SPLC 2016). The results of this report demonstrate that these social inequities have real consequences in the classroom and for our future students. Teacher preparation programs must be equipped to teach the critical consciousness required in our educators to minimize those inequities in the classroom and provide equitable access to high-quality education.

In light of a brief review of demographics and achievement trends of K-12 students, teachers, and post-secondary education programs, the history of teaching and education, the existing white supremacist policy in public education, the current context within our presidential administration, and the call for multicultural education to "level up," it is clear that there is a sense of urgency around global demographic shift and a need for culturally diverse teachers to provide a broader perspective to an inclusive student body.

In chapter 2, we discuss the role of teacher education, expanding the argument that the role of multicultural education as a pedagogical approach is inadequate for addressing these needs of the educational system. We expand upon the need for a paradigm shift in the awareness and emotional intelligence of teacher candidates and the importance of addressing the importance of developing these skills within teacher candidates to facilitate growth that surpasses current behavior and the development of a "personal self" and "teacher self." We provide examples of how to teach our teacher candidates about global competence, and why it is important, necessary, and crucial to equity and inclusion in our classrooms. We illustrate a detailed and comparative example of white supremacist curricula and a socially just curricula. Finally, we address the tendency of academia to lean on a teacher-centered lecture model and examine the role this plays in addressing a socially just curriculum.

In chapter 3, we discuss a study that was conducted in one author's teacher education classroom. Here, the instructor of the class collaborated with a colleague overseas to develop a pen pal email exchange that would build intercultural skills among teacher candidates. Results were measured by way of a Cultural Diversity Awareness Inventory, reflective prompts, email exchanges, post-graduation interviews, and performance assessments. The findings from this study are discussed in detail in addition to the conclusions that were drawn from the instructor's reflection, forming the impetus for this book.

In chapter 4, we define and discuss Critical Race Theory, intersectionality, giving voice to the voiceless, and defining and acknowledging the voice of color. We discuss the role of Critical Race Theory in education and teacher preparation. We examine the idea that "American" does not mean "White," and discuss ideas about retraining preservice teachers to critically analyze curricula through the lens of the marginalized.

In chapter 5, we examine the question "what are the steps to interrupting the cycle of white supremacist curricula in the educational system?" We provide recommendations to teacher educators and for preservice programs and professional development of in-service teachers. Lastly, we acknowledge that national legislative measures may not lead policy change, and provide rationale for our call for public education institutions, administrators, and state agencies to create long-overdue policy that responds to the social and cultural change.

*Chapter 2*

# The Role of Teacher Education

## MULTICULTURAL EDUCATION AS A PEDAGOGICAL APPROACH IS INADEQUATE

Established in the 1980s, Multicultural Education was touted as the answer to the academic divide in public schools. Disproportionality between the academic outcomes of mostly white suburban schools and the urban schools serving students of color was alarming and apparent. Legislative fixes to this disproportionality came in the introduction of high stakes standardized testing and punitive consequences for schools failing to meet the expectations (Ravitch, 2010). Educators looked for pedagogical answers for why students of color were failing these assessments without addressing the social factors of privilege and marginalization. Well-meaning educators practiced simulated tolerance as they took on the charge of multicultural education in the name of "doing good" for the children, without examining their own bias, and this role furthered the systemic oppression of underrepresented populations. The standardization and centralization of curriculum testing silence the myriad of nonwhite voices that speak knowledge and truth. Knowledge and truth, therefore, are defined by a limited scope of those with cultural and social capital. Viewing knowledge and truth through a myopic lens forces one set of answers. This limited viewpoint silences the voices of the oppressed and fabricates consent and cohesion among all peoples. In the case of public schools in the United States, the Eurocentric perspective is the only perspective that is valued as truth and knowledge (Bigelow, 2014). High stakes standardized tests not only assess student knowledge through a Eurocentric lens, but they beget "teaching to the test" which directs instruction to follow the same path. This viewpoint also forces students to memorize facts as seen by the authority of the state while preventing the other perspectives, learning styles, and cultural knowledge from being heard, honored, and cultivated. In contrast, the goals of multicultural education attempt to highlight injustices and access multiple perspectives toward solutions. Ideally, if implemented appropriately, it instructs students on their responsibility to each other and the planet (Bigelow, 2014).

Multicultural education was defined at the time to be the path to assisting students of color to positive academic outcomes in their underfunded, dilapidated buildings with unlicensed teachers, absence of textbooks, and limited programming (Ravitch, 2010). Multicultural education became the "thing" and not the process it was intended to be (Ladson-Billings, 2004).

In its inception, Hollinger (1995) described Black, Latino/a, Asian, and Indigenous peoples' inequity and marginalization as an "ethno racial pentagon" that comprises the foundations of US culture (Ladson-Billings, 2004). Foucault's writing on social control and governmental regulations argues that culture is created through the process of marginalization of certain identities (1991). Educators and policymakers in support of the multicultural lens in public education attempted to address both the representation and curriculum concerns with the onset of "dedicating" a month to marginalized identities; that is, Black History Month, Women's History Month, Hispanic History Month, without ever addressing the social forces that marginalize people of color. For example, addressing the history of Black people for 28 days a year does not impact the phenomenon of "driving while Black" in America. Multicultural education cannot be seen as inclusion and representation of "the other"; instead, it must be seen as a process of analysis of the cultural practices that impact all humans (Ladson-Billings, 2004).

The attempted attainment of cultural agency reaches as far back as James Baldwin and W. E. B. DuBois and their attempts to position Black people as full cultural agents within their existence. Social movements in the 1960s and 1970s strained existing laws and constructed new legislation using the language of civil rights forcing the poor, women, and people of color to be recognized for their humanity (Ladson-Billings, 2004). As Multicultural Education evolved in the 1990s and 2000s, schools developed a programming feature that included marginalized knowledge and inclusion. Most obvious are the months dedicated to the history of one marginalized identity, the specific academic pursuits of specialized social sciences such as ethnic studies, gender studies, African American history courses, and others. From this structured programming of diversity, three branches of multiculturalism developed: conservative/corporate, liberal, and left-liberal multiculturalism. According to Ladson-Billings (2004), these branches became the collateral subsets of curricula aligned to the marginalized knowledge and inclusion (Ladson-Billings, 2004).

Conservative/corporate multiculturalism repudiates racism, marginalization, and privilege. These concepts are fervently denied to exist in US society (Ladson-Billings, 2004). Instead, this subset insists that we are a society that rewards individuals on merit alone. The meritocracy is uplifted as true freedom while denying that class, gender, race, or religious privilege exists. Multiculturalism is narrowed to having women and people of color present in board rooms, offices, and governmental roles. These positions are narrowed to the appearance of inclusion and often disparagingly referred to as "token minorities" or "quota hirings."

Liberal multiculturalism emphasizes sameness and inclusion without dismantling the current power dynamic and privilege in society (Ladson-Billings, 2004). This subset values an environment free of discrimination and concepts of being treated with sameness in every aspect, regardless of the agency of the people liberal multiculturalism is attempting to support. This is also referred to as "allyship." For example, a white female uses her privilege to stand up for her Muslim coworker in the face of office perpetuated microaggressions. In this scenario, the white "ally" is using her agency to silence the voice of the marginalized coworker to demand that she be treated the same. In most cases, the white "ally" is not cognizant that the needs of the marginalized coworker cannot be met by the needs of the white female coworker, these needs must be met by the employer. Through these actions, the "ally" is not actually impacting the power dynamic in play at the office. Instead, she is pointing out the discrimination at the expense of the agency of the marginalized coworker.

Left-liberal multiculturalism upholds "otherness" as alluring and mysterious, and its hallmark is a reliance on separate and unique programming for particular identities without addressing the intersectionality of these identities and their impact on the quality of life (Ladson-Billings, 2004). Like liberal multiculturalism, this subset focuses on the uniqueness of the "other." For example, gender studies in higher education often address the patriarchy and the oppression in the forms of sexism and toxic masculinity. However, these courses and programs often fail to address the complexities in the lives of women of color, transgender identities, Latin X, heteronormativity, and sex workers/slaves.

A large number of academic scholars studying the effectiveness of Multicultural Education (Allard, 2006; Ladson-Billings and Tate, 1995; Mohanty, 1994) have demonstrated the inadequacies in this pedagogy to remediate race-based academic disproportionality. According to Sheets, the difficulties schools and teachers have in moving from theory to practice are often not analyzed (2003). The research fails to address the gaps between theory and practice (Ngo, 2010). This movement toward a multicultural educational pedagogy and practice of its tenets failed to repair the academic outcomes of people of color in public schools. According to the National Center for Educational Statistics 2011 Achievement Gap Report, nationwide statistics demonstrate that Black students maintain an academic achievement gap of thirty-one points in eighth-grade math compared to white students. For students identified as Hispanic, there is a twenty-one-point gap in academic outcomes in fourth and eighth-grade math compared to white students. In reading, fourth-graders nationwide who identify as Hispanic had a twenty-six point gap from their white peers and a twenty-five point gap in eighth grade (NCES, 2015). These results inform teacher preparation programs and pedagogical scholars to the ineffectiveness of this form of multicultural education. The marginalized inclusion and knowledge of "other" cultures are not meeting the needs of all students in the public school system. Many educators take up multicultural education in the frame of America being a nation of diverse immigrants while covering up and/or ignoring the systemic oppression of class, race, national origin, religion, gender identities, heteronormativity, and citizenship status (Au, 2014).

In a research study completed in 2010 of one high school in the Midwest, Ngo reported on data revealing that at this specific location, multicultural education maintained the status quo and oftentimes escalated problems related to difference, which in turn resulted in teachers feeling skeptical and resistant to multicultural reform efforts. At the same time, the research illuminates how focusing on the tensions, power relations, and conflicts that exist in cultural differences may offer a clearer pathway to implementing the goals of social justice in multicultural education (Ngo, 2010). The school-wide efforts to recognize cultural differences escalated intense curricular debates on what counts as "knowledge" and how different cultures should be represented and taught (Cornbleth and Waugh, 1995). The attempt to acknowledge the existence of numerous groups and cultures plays out most frequently within the overarching philosophy of "multiculturalism." As a political philosophy of "many cultures" (Ladson-Billings and Tate, 1995), multiculturalism attempts "to subsume this plurality of cultures within the framework of a national identity" (Gupta and Ferguson, 1997, p. 35; Ngo, 2010).

Educational pedagogical theorists have identified three problems with this "stomp and chomp" (Allard, 2006, p. 328) approach to multicultural education. First, it focuses on "healing past wounds" (Mohanty, 1994) of violence and exclusion. Marked by efforts of "inclusion" and inclusion in the form of "celebration," this approach invalidates the histories of power inequities, of real harm and oppression (Burbules, 1997; Mohanty, 1994; West, 2002). By focusing on "making peace" with the past, it ignores institutionalized oppression and a power dynamic that sustains societal inequity. Furthermore, multicultural education in practice ignores the socialization process of people that creates bias and stereotypes to these cultural differences (Ngo, 2010).

Second, the importance of themes of "appreciation" or "celebration" in multicultural education results in the simplification of cultural differences into categories to which the dominant hegemony can "tolerate." The cultural difference becomes ceremonial and acknowledged in isolated "tolerance units," "multicultural weeks," or "history months." This claim to honor and "celebrate diversity" positions and reinforces difference as "exotic," something to be viewed in a condescending lens of "cute and quaint" (Burbules, 1997). Here, culture is actualized on a special day, month, week, and glamorized. This celebration of unfamiliar people, food, music, clothes, customs, among other things, sustains the power rankings of the privilege of the dominant hegemony and the marginalization of the "other" (Ngo, 2010). Finally, the focus of multicultural education is often on teaching the values of empathy, respect, understanding, and tolerance of differences in cultural norms. The rationale states, "If I can see things from your point of view, I can assimilate it into my own lived experience and knowledge." This is problematic because the assumption that one can easily know the experience of oppression felt by people of color, transgender, people of the Jewish faith, and others is questionable due to one's own identity privilege. Additionally, knowing this experience and feeling empathy for it will not deconstruct the institutionalized oppression that people of marginalized identities experience in society or in the classroom. This empathetic knowledge will not secure equitable access to high-quality education or academic outcomes for all students. Comparatively, Multicultural Education was designed to be a movement of change to remediate educational inequality by reforming educational practice. However, in practice, it often fails to live up to its goals of social justice (Ngo, 2010).

In the research outcomes of the high school in the Midwest, conflict among students and skepticism among teachers was not addressed by this reform movement. The research suggests that the focus on ceremony and conciliation did not work for students or teachers. A lack of critical approaches to multicultural education impacted the attitudes of teachers entrusted to enact these reform practices in their instructional strategies. For the students, the multicultural education efforts failed to address all identities. This left students to face homophobia, racism, and ethnic tensions in their learning communities without support or instruction (Ngo, 2010).

Students need Multicultural Education that is grounded in the lives they experience as their own identity, that draws on the perspectives of the people being studied, engages students in dialogue, provides a critical analysis of all identities, embraces and recognizes the native languages of students, critiques knowledge that is Eurocentric, facilitates social and political issues through dialogue, inspires participation in learning communities that is inclusive and democratized, uplifts academic rigor, connects and aligns to entire curricula, is rooted in anti-racist struggle, fights against nativism, xenophobia, and white supremacy, and deconstructs the sociopolitical institutions that contribute and uphold inequality (Au, 2014). Multicultural education must shift from a concept of diversity to actively anti-racist practices with the inclusion of socially just content in the educational curricula. Diversity is a noun in social vernacular used to name equity or the appearance of equity. Anti-racist and socially just education is a verb. It is an action taken by educators to minimize the oppressive social forces in their classrooms and create an inclusive and democratized space where students have access to high-quality education.

Within the confines of the teacher preparation programs provided nationwide by public and private colleges and universities, their current pedagogies play a key and intentional role in maintaining this substandard schooling and racial subjugation faced by Black and Brown students in public education and society (Harris, Hayes, and Smith 2020). Within public schools, Whiteness is reflected in the curricula, teaching and assessment practices, teacher-student interactions, decision making and is consistent with the privileging of the interests, values, accomplishments, and histories of white people. Harris, Hayes, and Smith illuminated in their research on teacher preparation programs the pervasive Whiteness that exists in, what they refer to as, pedagogical moments. Their research highlights ten specific moments in which pervasive Whiteness and interest convergence exist within the teacher preparation programs. The research suggests that the Whiteness of education and the preparation of teachers for Whiteness is actualized when white colleagues emphatically insist that, as a program, school, or college, we, as educators, have always been racially integrated while constructing a diversity plan or committee. Another pedagogical moment, according to these researchers, is when a failure to enact a socially just curricula occurs. There is a prominent lack of Black, Indigenous, LatinX, women educators or methods courses within these programs. The lack of Black, Indigenous, People of Color (BIPOC) faculty within teacher preparation programs is mirrored by the recruiting strategic search committees. These committees search for BIPOC faculty that will uphold white ideals. Professional interactions and decision-making processes that address racialized discussion or race work are found to be offensive by colleagues within these programs and are frequently avoided. As an extension, faculty and colleagues find it rude to focus on the pervasive educational and societal inequities within the United States. Another pedagogical moment is the upholding and protecting of the feelings of white faculty and colleagues over the racialized harm being done to Black and Brown students in public education. Teacher preparation programs often forget that the faculty are (supposedly) there for the students, not the other way around. When white colleagues speak about what they learned on international trips, alternative spring breaks, or reference personal narratives regarding being friends with or interactions with Black and Brown folx, they fail to see the perspective that taking one's white body into socially "othered" spaces does not make one an expert on culture and inclusion.

One of the most destructive pedagogical moments that embed white supremacy within teacher education is when white colleagues and faculty insist that the root of social inequity is socioeconomic class and not race. An extension of this is when colleagues and faculty protest against explicit talk and action taken against injustices and inequity in education and society. Another harmful pedagogical moment that maintains the status quo of white supremacy is the self-congratulatory group or individual conversations around "how much we have improved" that are allowed to overshadow the current issues facing Black and Brown folx. The final pedagogical moment discovered by Harris, Hayes, and Smith within teacher preparation programs is that colleagues and faculty are indignant and outraged that the program's official efforts, endeavors, and awards are questioned and criticized. The expectation is to focus on the good being done for Black and Brown students and should be above reproach (Harris, Hayes, and Smith 2020).

## THE AWARENESS OF TEACHER CANDIDATES: BEYOND BEHAVIOR

As stated in the previous chapter, the racial and ethnic makeup of teachers in the public school setting are overwhelmingly white and female. Racial minorities make up about 17 percent of the total US K-12 faculty. In teacher preparation programs nationwide, 83 percent of faculty in teacher education programs are white, while Black teachers (6.6 percent) make up the second largest group of full-time faculty and instructional staff in education programs (US Department of Education, National Center for Education Statistics, 2005).

Volumes of academic research support findings that suggest students with marginalized identities have been found to resist a hegemonic indoctrination of Eurocentric education and schooling historically (Freire 1970; Delpit 1996; Nieto 2004; McLaren 1989; Fordham and Ogbu 1986; Fine 1991). From this research, there is a clear call for the need for effective and unique instructional strategies to engage students with marginalized identities in their own learning (Evans-Winters and Hoff, 2011). Hence, the development of special education models like Response to Intervention (RtI) and Multicultural Education was formed to address the learning "problems" of students of color. This resulted in an overrepresentation of marginalized students in special education, increased dropout rates, and over usage of the label "at-risk" at the K-12 level.

Comparatively, white student resistance in higher education, and specifically teacher preparation programs, to alternative ways of knowing and analyzing within the world is inferred to be innocent and non-threatening to their own academic achievement, professional growth, and career outcomes of faculty in teacher preparation programs (Evans-Winters and Hoff, 2011). This is problematic because white teacher candidates' resistance is ignored by the faculty of these teacher preparation programs, because they maintain a lack of awareness for teacher candidates who look and act like them, as there is a shared privilege and ignorance to the implicit biases they both hold. A failure to address these issues in the preparation of becoming an educator leads to marginalized students being harmed by their teachers.

King (1991) used the term "dysconscious racism" to explain white students' resistance to her social foundations course (Evans-Winters and Hoff, 2011). King explains that

> dysconsciousness is an impairment of the consciousness brought on by the internalization of uncritical perceptions, beliefs and values that maintain unequal racialized power relations. Dysconscious racism, a form of racism is ontologically teethed to white supremacy which prevents students from distinguishing between racist justifications that maintain the racialized status quo and their own biases. Courses and/or dialogues which aggravate and challenge these deeply held convictions are met with resistance expressed as guilt and hostility. (p. 464)

Tatum (1992) asserts that white students are overexposed to white supremacy that predicates the internalization of stereotypes and bias. In 1997, Tatum constructed a model in an attempt to further understand the ways racism is replicated in the mind. Identifying that white supremacist ideology along a lifespan makes their resistance seem like cultural predominance, that is, "the way we've always done things" (Evans-Winters and Hoff, 2011). Teacher candidates need explicit teaching of white supremacy, Eurocentric curriculum, marginalization, and privilege must be addressed in order to counteract this lifespan of privilege and ignorance that contribute to the inequitable social forces at play in their future students' lives. White people raised in Western cultures are accustomed to white supremacist perspectives because it comprises the foundations of our society and sociopolitical institutions. Without addressing these issues, the messages we give to students, such as "everyone is equal," hanging posters indicating the value of diversity in the halls of their high schools, are null and void (Diangelo, 2018). How many people of color they know, befriend, or work with, and/or the marginalized people in their families, the message of white supremacy is everywhere (Diangelo, 2018). Teacher preparation programs must acknowledge this in their teaching and demonstrate to students how to identify it. This racial status quo is very comfortable for white people and there is no progress without discomfort. This power differential is historical and normalized. Racism differs from prejudice because of its accumulation throughout history and its embedding into our sociopolitical institutions (Diangelo, 2018). Teacher candidates must fully experience this to know it and bring awareness to privilege. In their acknowledgment of race, class, gender, sexual, and religious privilege, the preparation of the educator moves beyond a cognitive awareness to behavior change.

Using a Critical Race Theory lens to teach the principles of Multicultural Education is the remedy of reform for the disproportional academic outcomes for students with marginalized identities. In teacher preparation programs, it is essential that the societal forces of privilege and oppression experienced by each identity are explicitly taught through a Critical Race Theory framework for teacher candidates to identify marginalizations within the institution of public education and their own classrooms. As Beverly Daniel Tatum explains in her article, *Teaching White Students About Racism,* there are really only three models of Whiteness available to students within which they are able to identify. The actively racist white supremacist, the deniers that Whiteness is a racialized category that carries personal significance, and the shameful white person who knows it exists but lives in the guilt feelings of association that can be paralyzing (Tatum, 2009). However, there is another model that exists for white students to identify. The active anti-racist also known as the "white ally" or the social justice "co-conspirator" is a white person with knowledge of racism and more importantly, race privilege. This ally/co-conspirator will intentionally access their white privilege to work against white supremacy. Information about white people who work to intentionally dismantle white supremacy can look like; that is, white professors teaching about racism, white leaders of grassroots social movements working to end white supremacy, historical white leaders of Abolitionist and Civil Rights movements. This model is as important to the development of white racial identity just as much as the representation of empowered people of color is to marginalize identities (Tatum, 2009) and is the antithesis of the neoliberal multiculturalism because the "ally" is not removing the agency of her coworker.

## TEACHING GLOBAL COMPETENCE THROUGH A CRITICAL RACE THEORY LENS

One way in which educators take a multicultural frame in their teaching is to focus on the globalization movement and market. Public education is currently adopting a global perspective in order to prepare students to interact in a global economy as an equal citizen. In response, many universities are offering semesters abroad, alternative spring breaks, and international summer courses that allow their students to interact in the world as a global citizen. For teacher candidates, many of these opportunities are educationally based. A few examples include a teacher candidate who may spend an alternative spring break in Guatemala teaching six and seven-year-old children to speak English, a teacher candidate can take an educational course in China or Ireland in the summer through a partnership between universities, and some teacher candidates will have an opportunity to spend a semester in Germany taking teacher preparation courses in their School of Education. For teacher candidates, especially, many programs offer immersion experiences as a way to provide such an opportunity for their students or provide student teaching in globally disparate areas, such as programs offered by x, y, z university. More often than not, teachers do what they can with what they have, as exemplified in chapter 3. In a global economy, we strive to educate teacher candidates on how to deal with others in the world. How students are taught in the classroom should model their future work world. The majority of students in these programs will work with students with multiple identifiers that are both privileged and marginalized. In order for universities to prepare teacher candidates for this global economy, they need to pay particular importance to the inequality between countries. As professors, we cannot continue to ignore the oppression and systemic discrimination happening globally, that is, Malaysia, where civil rights are not spoken of.

Transnational scholarship introduces us to the ways in which oppression is shaped by geography, history, and international relations. The critical examination of global economics and its impact on labor, migration, gender, and ethnicities differs across the globe. Embracing a global perspective supports an intention to critically analyze how policies and organized coalitions (EU, UN, WHO, etc.) can meet the needs of people in different locations and contexts (Bell, 2016). Colonialism and Imperialism are the most obvious examples of cultures dominated from an external entity. For these countries, political power lies outside the country's culture and is imposed on those being colonized. The ways in which this power is imposed can vary, however, typically, the construction and enforcement of law and the broad mechanisms of social and economic control are at the source of colonialism. These impositions can be direct from the colonizer or implemented through the local agencies (Grant, 1997). The apartheid of South Afrikaans, in which the Dutch installed a system of apartheid to control and oppress the native culture of that country, is an excellent example of the broad mechanisms used in addition to the legislative power used to control the behavior and access of the colonized.

A system of public education will develop a foundation of cultural norms that naturally reflect the norms of the dominant or ruling society, and those few in number will have to adapt. This group of people must learn the language and the cultural norms of the dominant society to be able to function. For this group, the struggle becomes the degree to which adaptation is required and to what extent their own culture can be saved. Current examples of this are present in South Africa, North Africa, India, and others. The educational system is then faced with questions such as "to what extent should they take cultural differences into account?" and "how much variation is acceptable?" Should the educational system seek to assimilate the marginalized group or encourage and develop their own cultures, or something in between? Multicultural educational policy tends to focus on specific problems, language development, and literacy, rather than the influence the colonizer has on curriculum which leads to assimilation, domination, and control (Grant, 1997).

Multicultural and transnational issues have absolute implications for the education of privileged and marginalized students. Cultural diversity will not solve the problems of the power hierarchy in a colonized environment. The social constructs and attitudes of the dominant group on sex roles, the balance of rights between the individual and the family or community, or even the value of life or may conflict with the norms and laws maintaining the marginalization in that location. Dominant cultures, however, may become aware of identity but do not usually suffer from systemic-based problems because of their identities. Another way of dominating another culture through education is the inclusion of missionary or church schools into the colonized territory, an approach used widely in the British-ruled territories of Africa and on the Indigenous tribes of colonial America. Historically, policies of assimilating the identity of these groups have been by far the most common and harmful (Grant, 1997), and the process of this assimilation can be referred to as "minoritization." An example of this issue that regularly plays out within the American Public Education system, is that of a shift in leadership within the family. Before North America was colonized by the Spanish, French, and British, the communities were matriarchal in nature. Through colonization and dominance, the Western colonizers established communities, and later founded a country based on patriarchy that more closely matched their own native culture.

The tenets of Critical Race Theory will broaden the lens of the teacher candidate to understand the role education can play in colonization, inequitable power structures, and oppression. The first of these tenants is to understand that racism exists and is the foundation of our society. The second feature explains that racism is hard to eradicate because of the interest convergence of white elites and the white working class who benefit from the marginalization of Black and Brown folks. Social construction of identities and labels is the third feature of Critical Race Theory which is closely connected to the fourth feature of intersectionality of identities that create complexities in managing life. The final tenant of Critical Race Theory is honoring the voices of the marginalized. Voices of color hold credibility because of their expertise in the lived experience (Delgado and Stefancic, 2001).

Application of these tenets of Critical Race Theory in concert with the Multicultural Framework of globalization allows educators to truly prepare students for a globalized economy. Globalization has real impacts on international economies. Globalizing the economy can alter the location of manufacturing jobs from urban centers, create technologies, and informational industry jobs for which few people in the marginalized group are trained. This movement concentrates capital into pockets only the elite class can access. Critical Race theorists will argue that the situation of domestic workers in Third World countries is not much different than the labor opportunities for undocumented people or people with marginalized identities within the United States working in the same industry, as both of these industries employ poor, formerly colonized people, people of color, and mostly women (Delgado and Stefancic, 2001).

Immigration law is an aspect of globalization that needs a critical race analysis. The United States tolerates and sometimes supports the oppressive regimes in countries where the United States has previously stolen its wealth and resources through colonization. In order to flee the oppression, poverty, and violence, citizens of these countries want to immigrate to the United States. Because of the plenary power doctrine, Congress has virtually unlimited power in regulating immigration. The treatment of these potential immigrants cannot be challenged in the courts resulting in harsh treatment to those fleeing oppression (Delgado and Stefancic, 2001). This makes one consider how American society would treat its own people of color if the courts were not regulating civil rights.

## HOW TO IDENTIFY WHITE SUPREMACIST CURRICULA COMPARED TO A SOCIALLY JUST CURRICULA

To view the current state of public education curricula as the colonizer indoctrinating the colonized would not be incorrect. The use of standardized testing that is standardized to white, male, middle class, Christian culture leaves students that do not hold those identities (the colonized) at a great disadvantage when measuring academic outcomes (Ravitch, 2010). It is not enough for teacher candidates to comprehend the tenets of Critical Race Theory, access the Critical Race Theory framework in their pedagogical practice, and uphold the goals of multicultural education. Teacher candidates must be able to supplement socially just curricula with the curricula of the dominant hegemony. In order to balance the curricula between the dominant or school-sponsored curriculum and supplement with the socially just content, teacher candidates must be able to identify white supremacist curricula and dismantle it.

Today's public school curricula create learning environments that not only miseducate white students but leave students with marginalized identities feeling as if their identities are being attacked (Au, 2014). Multicultural education is founded in the anti-racist struggle over whose knowledge and experiences get to become the public school curricula. In March of 2010, The Texas Board of Education gave initial approval for new standards that would align with conservative thinking in regards to history and economics. These new standards would emphasize the superiority of American capitalism, question the thinking of the founding members of the US government in wanting a secular society, and present Republican political philosophies in a more positive light by claiming these political philosophies as patriotism (Bigelow, 2014). At the same time, the Texas Board of Education eliminated the content of the 1848 Seneca Falls Women's Rights Declaration and made it a legal requirement to teach the Inaugural address of Confederate president Jefferson Davis alongside Lincoln's Inaugural Address. At the time of publication, there were 100 amendments made to the 120 page social studies curriculum. These amendments ensured that there was no recognition of current social issues such as the inequitable and unsustainable world, ecological crisis, or poverty. The standards portray US society as congruous with laws that ensure equity and progress. These standards support the myth of meritocracy and concepts of racism, classism, sexism, and oppression are not mentioned (Bigelow, 2014). In the same year two states to the West, Arizona, passed a House Bill 2281 that states,

> the Arizona legislature finds and declares that public school pupils should be taught to treat and value each other as individuals and not be taught to resent or hate other races or classes of people . . . to promote the overthrow of the United States Government. (HB 2281)

This bill was designed to eliminate the Mexican-American Studies Program at Tucson Unified School District (TUSD), essentially making ethnic studies in the State of Arizona illegal. According to the state legislature, the only permitted curriculum was Euro-centered or white studies. The students of TUSD protested and marched against this oppression of knowledge and in 2017, a federal judge ruled the law as unconstitutional. In his ruling, the judge explicitly acknowledged the state's discriminatory intent to outlaw Mexican-American History (Carberry, 2014). Those who promoted HB 2281 didn't want students thinking in terms of race, class, ethnicity, or solidarity. The strategic manipulation of the law to ensure that only white supremacy is taught in public schools cannot go unnoticed or unanswered. The common thread in the oppressive actions taken by Texas and Arizona toward its young people is the disrespect those in power have for students' abilities to think individually, critically, and act based on their learning. This type of Whitewashing is not limited to educational policy, as curriculum materials are also Euro-centered and support white supremacy. Bigelow examined eight children's biographies of Columbus to account for accuracy to the historical record and its influence on young people. The biographies had similar themes for young people reading their contents. The biographies (1) hailed Columbus as a hero and adventurer; (2) Represented the lives of those who labored for Columbus on his voyages as wretched, or left out representations of their lives altogether; (3) Justified colonialism and racism as needed for progress; (4) Represented foreign policy as synonymous to inequity in world power; (5) Did not express outrage at the social (genocide and slavery) and economic (stealing of resources and land attainment) systems represented in Columbus's behaviors toward the indigenous people; and (6) Uplifted Columbus as the discoverer of a "New World" instead of showing how he contributed to the inventions of slavery and colonialism (Bigelow, 2014). The teaching of Columbus as a heroic figure in public schools is only one example of how colonization, enslavement, and genocide in the name of wealth, progress, and greed is a part of the American way of life. The void of curricular perspectives from the enslaved, indigenous, or even Columbus's crew itself provides no foundation for a meaningful discussion of the power dynamics, oppression, and cruelty. By not including these perspectives in the text, young children may be left with the understanding that oppression is an appropriate way to gain wealth, status, and power, yet each year, most students celebrate his cruelty and greed with a day off school or a day designated to his "accomplishments."

Mixing a social justice educational approach with a multicultural/diversity education model allows for discussions of marginality, inequity, and oppression to be interwoven with the representation and celebration of cultural differences. One goal of social justice education is to engage all people in recognizing the harm and collateral damage caused by maintaining systems of oppression (Bell, 2016). Using a combination of the social learning pedagogy, social psychology pedagogy and educational reform pedagogy with pedagogies that encompass approaches that are activist, conscience raising, and that support social movement such as those from Paulo Freire, Lisa Delpit, bell hooks, and Gloria Ladson-Billings will frame the teaching practices of educators. These pedagogies will inform instructional strategies and create inclusive learning environments. Teachers that work for social justice in their learning environments follow the steps in figure 2.1.

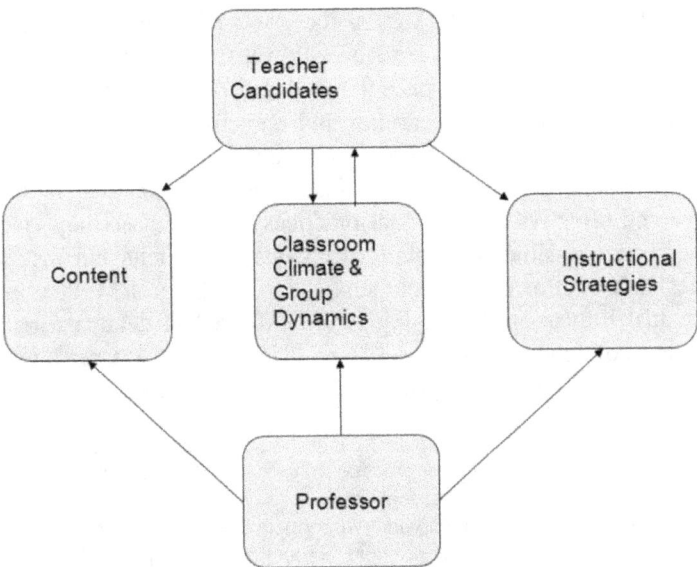

Figure 2.1   Adapted from Bell, Goodman, and Ouelett, 2016.

## TEACHER PREPARATION PROGRAMS PERPETUATE WHITE SUPREMACY

Teacher preparation programs perpetuate the status quo of teaching by modeling an outdated teacher-centered lecture model. The majority of professors unintentionally perpetuate this Eurocentric educational model in their courses by basing their curricular content on state standards for curricula (Texas and Arizona) and state teacher certification requirements. The methods of teaching in higher education fail to model democratization of a learning space or student-centered teaching. The use of a lecture format allows for no dialogue between students or between students and teacher, only a monologue where the professor is the expert and therefore should be the only voice heard in the room unless you have a question (Au, 2014). Overall the majority of teacher preparation programs have one required course on diversity and/or multicultural education. These required diversity courses may discuss racism, privilege, and social issues in a general way but fail to critically deconstruct the painful and powerful systemic racism people of color face in society or in public education, the US history of colonization, genocide, and human rights abuse, and the consequences of cultural oppression on individuals (Au, 2014).

The goal of multicultural education creates space for students to engage with one another in a meaningful way around real social issues. This inherently connects to learning outside the classroom and connecting with the world's cultures (Au, 2014). Adding the goals of social justice education to the multicultural education tenants within a framework of Critical Race Theory will create a learning space that is democratized. For educators seeking an inclusive and equitable learning environment, one must be mindful and strategic to the five dynamics present in the classroom (figure 2.2).

The professor in a teacher preparation program should be modeling inclusive and effective instructional practices in each class they teach. The professor is responsible for making decisions on content and instructional strategies, and both of these are crucial in the teaching of Multicultural and Socially Just Education. These topics are explored in detail earlier in this chapter and continued in chapter 4. Here, we focus on instructional strategies. The current lecture model of teaching perpetuates the white supremacist

| | |
|---|---|
| Teacher mindset | Teacher practices of inclusion and democratizing the classroom space. |
| Develop a critical consciousness | Develop an awareness in their students of the sociopolitical factors that create and sustain oppression by identifying it in the content being taught. |
| Deconstruct binaries | Identify and deconstruct the binary categories that perpetuate oppression in the content being taught. |
| Draw on counter-narratives | Supplement the Eurocentric curricula with the voices of the targeted group and include their stories of resistance. |
| Analyze power | Continually ask students: "Who has the power here?" "Who is benefiting from this policy/situation/legislation?" "Who is being targeted?" |
| Identify interest convergence | Deepen the critical thinking of the stakeholders in the content and how they benefit. Identify the allies of privilege in an attempt to understand the strategies of resistance. |
| Make global connections | Connecting students to the content in a global perspective to ensure they are knowledgeable global citizens. |
| Build coalitions and solidarity | Use coalitions to bring together multiple ways of understanding the world; specific skills of empathic listening and self-reflection need to be specifically instructed. |
| Follow the leadership of oppressed people | Ensuring people from the subordinate group are present and heard when solutions are being constructed. That is, students need a voice in school policies. |
| Model accountable and responsible allyship | Modeling for students how to use privilege to be accountable and responsible for the marginalized in learning environments. |

*Source*: Adapted from Bell, 2016.

**Figure 2.2   SJE and MCE Combination of Pedagogical Approach.**

model of public education. Culturally relevant and socially just instructional strategies include integrating the five dynamics into each lesson (Bell et al., 2106). The class climate should be established in the introductory class with a set of cultural norms and expectations for how to have a successful semester. The group's dynamics will organically develop in the first few weeks, and the professor will need to be mindful and purposeful with instructional strategies based on that dynamic. Professors must teach this content using four pathways of learning; (1) concrete experience, (2) reflective observation, (3) abstract conceptualization, and (4) active experimentation. Each instructional strategy must contain one or more of these pathways to learning for teacher candidates (Bell et al., 2016).

Integrating the work of early learning and teaching pedagogists, learning must impact the student cognitively, effectively, and kinesthetically to deepen comprehension and stimulate action (Bell et al., 2016). Concrete experiences for students move students from hearing stories of others' experiences to living these experiences. These learning opportunities in pedagogical programs should include the powerful simulation of privilege and marginalization. For teacher candidates who mostly experience race privilege, the opportunity to experience racism in a real-world scenario offers a paradigm of marginality they have never understood before but that will be experienced by their students. One example of this type of learning is when the students (as heterosexuals) are instructed to answer questions about their sexuality that are commonly asked of homosexuals. This simulation of heteronormativity creates a paradigm shift in the ways that teacher candidates think about the experiences of the LGBTQAI+ community in heteronormative spaces. Creating these feelings of marginalization is essential in moving from awareness to action.

Reflective observation is a teaching strategy that requires some framing in Critical Race Theory and facilitation. After watching a documentary clip, a video, listening to music or spoken word, or after content is given, the instructor uses strategically scaffolded questions that students will reflect on and extend their thinking, using a collaborative approach in random or strategic groups or pairs. Questions such as (1) Who has the power in this scenario? (2) Whose voices are not heard? (3) How might this policy impact who has access to this resource? (4) What are the implications for public education? These scaffolded questions guide teacher candidates through a process that has the potential to create a critical consciousness they may not have accessed before.

Abstract conceptualization is necessary for teacher candidates to comprehend systems thinking. To comprehend the institutionalization of oppression and discrimination, teacher candidates must have a foundation of the Cycle of Socialization. Understanding how society develops stereotypes that often lead to policy, and institutionalized discrimination leading to the oppression of a target group. An example often used in a course taught by one of the authors is a recounting of the author's own experience of socialization during the Cold War. As a 1980s kid, the author provides examples of doing drills once a month to prepare students in anticipation of a Russian nuclear attack. School, media, and family all emphasized a suspicion and fear of the Russians and this bled into national and local policies that impacted young children's lives. This national fear of a Russian attack resulted in monthly drills in school where small children were required to hide under desks. Going through this process solidified a prejudice against Russians for the author and most children of the 1980s. Films like "Red Dawn," "Red Army," and "From Russia with Love" reflected, exacerbated, and impacted the national climate around Russians and communism, resulting in a national paranoia and stereotyping of Russian people and culture.

Active experimentation assists teacher candidates in applying this new knowledge. The most common form is a case study. In the author's course, she uses examples from school districts to address issues of marginalization, prejudice, and institutionalized racism. These case studies are connected to a template that scaffolds the thinking of the teacher candidate. Asking teacher candidates to identify the overall problem, some underlying beliefs/values that are in conflict, the stakeholders, challenges and opportunities for the school community, and possible equitable outcomes for the community provides them with an opportunity to explore perspectives of the case in detail, allowing students to apply their new learning to real-life problem-solving in a safe and structured environment. These case studies and templates are taken from *Case Studies on Diversity and Social Justice Education* by Paul C. Gorski and Seema G. Pothinin. An example of a case study that has been used is as follows.

## CASE 9.2: DATE AUCTION

During a student council meeting at Shadow Creek High School, Jonathan, the council president, introduced the possibility of hosting a fundraiser for a local youth homeless shelter. Historically, Shadow Creek High School's student body had been white and upper middle class. The school is located in a predominantly affluent suburb 20 miles from a major metropolitan city. However, as Jonthan reminded his classmates, the school's student population was growing increasingly diverse racially and economically. "I hate that people think we're just a bunch of rich White kids," he said. "Here's something we can do to change that perception." The council voted in favor of hosting the fundraiser, hoping also that their efforts would raise awareness among their classmates of the growing problem of youth homelessness in the area.

Once the vote passed, council members eagerly began brainstorming fundraising ideas. Their adviser, Mr. Hanson, believed in students taking ownership of their own projects, so he asserted his voice minimally during meetings. He listened to their conversation intently but provided only occasional guidance.

One student, Tanya, suggested holding a "date Auction" in which students could bid on an opportunity to go on a date with members of the senior class. Tanya had read online about another high school that had hosted a similar event. "It generated a lot of money," she explained, "and cost next to nothing." She added that the dates could be arranged to happen simultaneously in a local restaurant, ensuring student safety and mitigating any discomfort participants might experience. Another student, Terry, wondered aloud whether the restaurant could donate the meals so that all of the money they raised through the auction could be donated to the shelter. The students continued to discuss and plan the event with great enthusiasm. Rarely had they so quickly agreed on a program. "Our classmates are going to love this!" Jonathan said to a chorus of nods.

When the time came to identify volunteers who would be willing to be auctioned off and who would generate a lot of bidding interest, Tanya recommended Nate, a make student council member. "Everyone knows Nate and, more importantly, everybody *loves* Nate," Tanya said smiling. Nate agreed, joking that he would win the highest bids.

Chris, one of Nate's best friends, assed that Nate would probably get bids "from girls *and from guys*" who would want a date with him, eliciting laughs from several of the students in the room.

Nate responded, "Whatever! I'm not gay. Even if it's for charity, I'm quitting if a guy bids on me. That's just wrong!" While some council members continued to laugh, others changed the topic to restaurants that might be willing to donate meals.

As planning was wrapping and the meeting was coming to a close, Tanya asked Mr. Hanson if it would be all right for the student council to stipulate that bids would only be considered if made by "students of the opposite sex from the students we're auctioning off." She hoped that this stipulation would help them "avoid that kind of situation." The council members looked at Mr. Hanson, waiting for a response.

Students in the teacher preparation programs are asked to read this case study, which actually took place in a public school, and name the issue. This case study example is an explicit example of heterosexism at play in public education. Not addressing the historical reference to auctioning people to the highest bidder and its painful connection to the slave trade, the idea did not seem to occur to Mr. Hanson or the student council that students identifying as LGBTQAI+ would be left out or marginalized. Tanya even wanted to make heterosexism a policy of the fundraiser in requesting that Mr. Hanson ban all homosexual bids. Teacher candidates are then expected to identify the stakeholders—both direct and indirect. In this case study, direct stakeholders would be Mr. Hanson, Chris, Nate, Tanya, Jonathan, and all students at Shadow Creek High School. Indirect stakeholders include: students identifying as LGBTQAI+, school administrators, the restaurant owner, parents of all students, and all school faculty. Teacher candidates are asked to name the stakeholders and state their perspectives on this issue. This helps to activate their critical consciousness in analyzing power structures within this incident. Teacher candidates will then identify the challenges and opportunities in this specific case and develop an equitable outcome for this fundraiser. The use of the case study allows teacher candidates the practice of applying socially just practices in real-life incidents in public schools. Case studies addressing ableism, ethnicity/racism, heterosexism, sexism, classism, gender identity, language oppression (Standard English Dominance), religious oppression, and immigration oppression are weaved throughout the course content for teacher candidates to practice and apply their new critical consciousness.

## CLOSURE

In the 1980s, the educational community responded to the ever expanding achievement gap between white and Black/Brown students with the onset of Multicultural Education, which became the attempt to answer disproportionality in academic achievement in public schools. The focusing belief of which assumed that expanding teacher knowledge of other cultures would somehow trickle down to student achievement. This new trend in education came in three forms; conservative/corporate multicultural education, liberal multicultural education, and left-liberal multicultural education. Educational scholars identified the inadequacies of each type of multicultural education within teacher practice. As a practice, each form of multicultural education ignored the socialization process within our society that creates implicit and explicit bias resulting in stereotypes that then inform policy. These educational policies replicate the inequitable power dynamics that exist in society into the classroom. Multicultural education is treated in an abstract way to address the historical inequalities existing in society. Combining Social Justice Education with Multicultural Education will allow for education grounded in current life experiences. This combination moves teacher candidates beyond awareness and into a praxis where a strategic plan to minimize exclusivity and inequity in the classroom community. The symbiosis of these two pedagogies gives the teacher candidate the specific instructional strategies to minimize exclusivity and bias. Teacher preparation programs must offer these candidates a modeling of these inclusive strategies, concrete experiences of oppression, reflective observations around power dynamics, privilege, and marginalization, abstract conceptualizations of systems thinking to understand institutionalized oppression, and active experimentation in applying this new knowledge in safe environments for risk taking and failures.

Research indicates that teacher preparation programs that emphasize a focus on multicultural education and/or social justice education are failing to have tough conversations around current social inequities, bias, stereotypes, and institutionalized oppression. Without this practical and honest knowledge and an application of a CRT lens, teacher candidates become teachers that perpetuate social inequality and institutionalized oppression in their classrooms, never seeming to minimize that achievement gap.

*Chapter 3*

# A Classroom Study of a Well-Meaning Teacher Educator

Jessica S. Krim, Susan E. Breck, Elly Ong,
Rachel Demon, Leyla Kays, and Abriella Jones

### AN INQUIRY OF CULTURAL DIVERSITY AWARENESS IN AMERICAN TEACHER CANDIDATES

This mixed-methods study examines teacher candidates' beliefs about cultural awareness and diversity change over the course of a preservice foundation class. Teacher candidates were required to participate in a pen pal exchange with Malaysian college students and reflect over that process. Statistical analysis shows growth across three subgroups of the Cultural Diversity Awareness Inventory used to measure change in the pre and post condition: Creating Multicultural Environments Using Multicultural Methods and Materials, General Cultural Awareness, and the Culturally Diverse Family. Areas that showed no statistical difference from the pre and post condition include subgroups of Cross-Cultural Communication and Assessment. Findings allow authors to impact program curriculum and support prior research findings by Larke (1990) and make note of instances of simulated tolerance being present among preservice teacher candidates (Evans-Winters and Hoff 2011). Additionally, findings illustrate that one stand-alone class on diversity is insufficient to cause meaningful and lasting change.

### INTRODUCTION

At the K-12 public school level, teacher demographics in the United States are typically female, middle class, white, and monolingual, which contrasts starkly with the population of students of color in their classrooms. This number of non-white students has grown in the past decade (NCES 2018) and is predicted to continue growing. It has long been understood that "research has shown that no one teaching strategy will consistently engage all learners. The key is helping students relate lesson content to their own backgrounds" (Wlodkowski and Ginsberg 1995, 1). In current preservice teacher education classrooms, two pedagogical approaches are typically seen: Multicultural Education (ME) and Culturally Responsive Teaching (CRT). These approaches are intended to address the need for facilitation of learning for all students. ME refers to any form of education or teaching that incorporates the histories, texts, values, beliefs, and perspectives of people from different cultural backgrounds (edglossory.org 3.6.2016) and can be approached in a variety of ways based upon the interests and commitment of the educator. CRT is a pedagogy that "crosses disciplines and cultures to engage learners while respecting their cultural integrity. It accommodates the dynamic mix of race, ethnicity, class, gender, region, religion, and family that contributes to every student's cultural identity" (ASCD 1995).

While ME focuses on the pedagogy used to teach K-12 students, culturally responsive pedagogy is focused upon the teaching of in-service and teacher candidates. While, as Howard describes, culturally responsive pedagogy is "more than just a way of teaching or a simple set of practices embedded in curriculum lessons and units. Culturally relevant pedagogy embodies a professional, political, cultural, ethical, and ideological disposition that supersedes mundane teaching acts; it is centered in fundamental beliefs about teaching, learning, students, their families, and their communities, and an unyielding commitment to see student success become less rhetoric and more of a reality" (Howard 2010, 68). An early description of the responsibilities of teachers states that they are "cultural organizers," "cultural mediators," and "orchestrators of social contexts" (Diamond and Moore 1995; Gay 2010). These definitions of teacher responsibilities have specific significance in this study, as the demographics of the participants closely reflect the demographics of teachers nationwide; most are of the Caucasian race, middle-class socioeconomic status, and Christian faith.

Although these approaches have been intended to provide opportunities for all students, to create fairness within an unequal system, there is a gap that is present in ME, and this chapter intends to contribute to the body of research that aims to address this gap. Willis and Meacham (1996) state, "It is imperative therefore that teacher education courses not merely teach about multicultural education, but that they become multicultural environments" (40). The authors purport that part of this gap occurs in the way teacher candidates "compartmentalize," or practice simulated tolerance (Evans-Winters and Hoff 2011). This is the phenomenon seen when teachers willingly go into high needs areas to teach, but once there, still harbor negative beliefs about the students and the community, or they teach by way of a deficit model

(Waddell 2013). Compartmentalization is also seen when teacher candidates are taught in teacher preparation programs where teacher educators may often advise, "don't share too much" or "keep a professional boundary." This message is often (mis)interpreted by teacher candidates as they should hide themselves from their students, or that there should be a "teacher-self" and a "personal self." teacher candidates enrolled in the university say time and time again, "I would never treat any of my students poorly, they are just children," and then witnessed by an author to bullying a classmate who falls into the category of "other."

Mezirow (1997) emphasizes that transformative learning is rooted in the way human beings communicate and it is not exclusively linked with significant life events of the learner. The authors posit that if Mezirow's philosophy is accurate, there must be a personal transformation, or inner work, that is needed in order to make real change. Howard states, "We cannot fully and fruitfully engage in meaningful dialogue across the differences of race and culture without doing the work of personal transformation" (2006, 9). Through this combination of reflection and discourse, teacher candidates were able to make shifts in their world views which produced a more inclusive understanding of the world and their role as educators. By engaging teacher candidates in this hard work of personal transformation, we can get closer to the goal of what Samuels (2014) calls multicultural preparedness. This study attempts to do that and measure the outcome of the interventions implemented within.

## PROBLEM AND PURPOSE

The purpose of this study is to examine how American teacher candidates' beliefs about cultural awareness and diversity change over the course of a preservice foundation class. This study engages critically with the process of teacher preparation and how to facilitate cultural diversity awareness among American educators by following a preservice teacher population that mirrors the national demographics of in-service teachers. Educating teacher candidates of privilege about how to understand and acknowledge their privilege and implicit bias is important for them to be able to truly teach all students.

The period in which this study takes place is over the course of three semesters (2016–2017). This study examines the development of American teacher candidates as they complete a unit in which they learn about culture and school systems through a "pen pal" exchange with college students at a technological university in Malaysia. The American students were expected to complete the "Cultural Diversity Awareness Inventory" (CDAI), send and respond to emails, and complete weekly metacognitive journal reflections.

The CDAI is a tool developed by Henry (1986) to measure student responses using a Likert scale across five subgroups.

The overall goal of the study was to introduce multicultural preparedness and provide a foundation for all of the overlapping implications (Marshall 2014) into K-12 classrooms, by developing and facilitating use of critical reflection (Brookfield 2018, 1987) and to provide teacher candidates a pathway to CRT (Gay 2010). Growth and development were measured by the administering of a CDAI at the beginning and end of the course.

## CONTEXT/THEORETICAL FRAMEWORK

The setting in which this initial phase takes place is in an undergraduate course—Planning for Diverse Learners. Students are taught components of educational psychology, an examination of implicit bias, and foundations of the American educational system. During this course, a key experience used for this study is a pen pal exchange assignment. For this assignment, American students exchanged emails with Malaysian students based upon the learning of each other's cultures and everyday activities. Pen pal experience was paired with Brookfield's framework for reflection in adult learning.

Epstein's definition of "international education" is represented in this study; the participants were part of an "organized effort to bring together students and teacher-scholars from different nations to interact and learn about and from each other" (Marshall 2014) by way of a pen pal exchange. Pen Pals have long been utilized as an educational tool, and projects involving this approach have been proven to be effective in a number of contexts for learning about both language (Bohinski and Leventhal 2015; Larotta and Serrano 2012; Liaw 1998; Shandomo 2009) and cultural diversity (Wilfong and Oberhauser 2012; McMillon 2009; Eppley, Shannon, and Gilbert 2011; Walker Dalhouse and Dalhouse 2009; Haley 2012). It is very important to make note of the power difference between pen pals; while some projects pair language learners with master-level speakers (Larotta and Serrano 2012) or teacher candidates with young students (Eppley, Shannon, and Gilbert 2011; McMillon 2009; Walker Dalhouse and Dalhouse 2009; Wilfong and Oberhauser 2012), other studies aim to create a more equal learning environment, where both parties are on similar footing (Bohinski and Leventhal 2015; Haley 2012; Liaw 1998, 2001; Shandomo 2009). Our project most closely represents the second type of project described, where each pen pal is an expert in their area. In the pen pal exchange, Malaysian college students were experts in their culture, and the American college students involved in this project were experts in their culture. Throughout email exchanges about culture, Malaysian college students were able to learn about American culture and American teacher candidates were able to learn about Malaysian culture.

Brookfield is well known for reflective practice for adult learners. By utilizing prompts based upon this work, participants were encouraged to reflect in the areas of "assumption analysis," "contextual awareness," "imaginative speculation," and "reflective skepticism" as defined by Brookfield's practice. Samples of teacher candidate reflections in each of Brookfield's categories are as follows:

Reflection Area #1: Assumption analysis: This is the first step in the critical reflection process. It involves thinking in such a manner that it challenges our beliefs, values, cultural practices, and social structures in order to assess their impact on our daily proceedings. Assumptions are our way of seeing reality and to aid us in describing the order of relationships. The reflection questions for this area include: What assumptions did you have about your pen pal, and were they proven or disproven? How so? Why is this important to you?

Reflection Area #2: Contextual awareness: Realizing that our assumptions are socially and personally created in a specific historical and cultural context. Reflection questions for this area include: What is the everyday context for your pen pal? How is that similar or different to your everyday context? Why is this important?

Reflection Area #3: Imaginative speculation: Imagining alternative ways of thinking about phenomena in order to provide an opportunity to challenge our prevailing ways of knowing and acting. Reflection questions for this area include: How does this information impact your teaching? What connections can you draw between this experience and your current or future classroom? Why is this important?

Reflection Area #4: Reflective skepticism: Questioning of universal truth claims or unexamined patterns of interaction through the prior three activities—assumption analysis, contextual awareness, and imaginative speculation. It is the ability to think about a subject so that the available evidence from that subject's field is suspended or temporarily rejected in order to establish the truth or viability of a proposition or action. Reflection questions for this area include: What will you now do differently that will make a difference for students in your current or future classroom? How does this impact you as an educator? How does this impact your students?

The reflection component, prompts based on Brookfield's approach, in particular, were important parts of the teacher candidates' growth as it allowed them a way to process what they were learning as they developed friendships with their Malaysian pen pals.

## Chapter 3

# METHODOLOGY

This mixed-methods longitudinal study took place from 2015 to 2017 in a mid-sized, Midwest university. Participants in this study were seeking licensure in either elementary education, early childhood education, or special education. Some had just been admitted into their program, while others were taking this course as a prerequisite to their program.

Most of the participants had grown up in communities in which a large majority (if not all) of the inhabitants look similar to them, and they now attend college in an environment that reinforces this environment. The population of teacher preparation programs at our university models nationwide trends of in-service teachers remaining white, female, monolingual, and Christian. While they may have had significant experience with the experiences of peers who fall into the low-income bracket or who have special learning needs, they are simply not aware of the challenges that are faced by students of a different race, ethnicity, or religion, on a daily basis. In the school unit, 79.5 percent of the undergraduate students are female, and 73.6 percent of the undergraduate students are white (SIUE Fact Book 2019).

The average age of the eighty-three participants was twenty-one and ranged from eighteen to forty-seven years of age. The majority of the participants in this study were white ($n = 73$) and female ($n = 77$). The majority of participants ($n = 75$) stated that they had not received any other training in ME, but they ($n = 72$) have had experiences with individual(s) who lived in or had moved to the United States from another country. The participants were asked to assess the amount of diversity in their community where they were raised, within the following categories: none ($n = 18$), a little ($n = 31$), a moderate amount ($n = 26$), and a large amount ($n = 8$); as well as to assess the amount of diversity in their current community, using the same categories of none ($n = 4$), a little ($n = 28$), a moderate amount ($n = 35$), and a large amount ($n = 16$).

Institutional Research Review and approval was implemented during all semesters in which data was collected from participants. Students who were enrolled in each semester of the course were presented with an explanation of the study and the data that would be collected. Students had the opportunity to "opt" out of the study, and their work was not recorded as part of the findings. All surveys were identified by codes, so the instructor of the course did not know which student participated or did not, and which student provided which answers on the CDAI assessment. All findings are being reported in aggregate or using code names for students in the case of direct quotes.

## DATA ACQUISITION

The CDAI survey consisted of twenty-eight questions scored with a Likert scale that examined the participants' self-assessment about their beliefs, practices, and values about cultural diversity. The twenty-eight items are split into subgroups as follows: General Cultural Awareness (five questions), the Culturally Diverse Family (seven questions), Cross-Cultural Communication (four questions), Assessment (three questions), and Creating a Multicultural Environment using Multicultural Methods and Materials (nine questions). In addition to these twenty-eight items, the survey collected demographic information from the participants including age, gender, race, educational program, perceived diversity of high school and current living environment, previous experience with this topic of study, and frequency of experience with individuals from other nations. Since its inception in 1986 (Henry), the CDAI has been utilized in assessing cultural diversity awareness among teacher candidates in a variety of settings. Below we highlight several of these studies with a brief description of how the CDAI was implemented.

Larke's 1990 "Cultural Diversity Awareness Inventory: Assessing the Sensitivity of Preservice Teachers" reported CDAI results on fifty-one female elementary preservice teachers. Most of these participants were white (n = 46) and several Mexican Americans (n = 5). Authors sought to answer two primary research questions: How culturally sensitive are preservice teachers generally; and are preservice teachers more culturally sensitive in some areas than in others. Descriptive statistics were utilized to analyze CDAI scores. Key findings indicate two points of contradiction or cognitive conflict: (1) The degree of sensitivity varies greatly depending upon how the issue is viewed, with candidates marking neutral scores to items which posed a conflict of values. (2) Preservice teachers desired parental participation but still maintained the belief that parents knew little about assessing their children. Larke indicated that the additional findings that 78.5 percent of the preservice teachers did not accept the students' use of nonstandard English, 47 percent believed that sometimes racial statements should be ignored, and 75 percent of the students may shift as the program curriculum was completed by these students.

Brown's 2004 "What Precipitates Change in Cultural Diversity Awareness During a Multicultural Course—The Message or the Method?" utilized the CDAI to examine the impact of instructional approach on the cultural diversity awareness of teacher candidates using two different approaches to a stand-alone cultural diversity course. Participants in this study included 109 students midway through their program. Most of the participants were white (n = 100), and others were Black (n = 7), Asian American (n = 1), and Native American (n = 1). The first approach focused on several components, including developing a sense of community among students, while the second approach, following a traditional model, did not pay specific attention to creating a community in the classroom. The data analysis was conducted by using a two-tailed analysis of variance (ANOVA) to obtain the mean and standard deviation of each group's pre- and post-test scores, and a two-tailed multivariate analysis of variance (MANOVA) using time as the repeated measure to test for significant changes over time between the two groups. Brown's findings include a statistically significant difference between groups across all five subgroups of the CDAI, indicating that the instructional approach makes a difference in students' cultural diversity awareness. In particular, the most effective method of course instruction was to focus the initial eight classes on reducing resistance and provide students with self-examination opportunities.

Walker Dalhouse and Dalhouse's 2006 "Investigating white Preservice Teachers' Beliefs about Teaching in Culturally Diverse Classrooms" used the CDAI to study ninety-two white preservice elementary education majors as they sought to address the question "do preservice teacher beliefs change after exposure to a diversity seminar and field experience?" Preservice teachers attended one of two field experiences, each with 29 percent of the population being underserved populations. Teachers and administrators in both schools were noted to have met the state-designated requirements for multiculturalism as well as being recognized in the academic community as responsive to the needs of their culturally, ethnically, and linguistically diverse students (p.73). The seminar included readings and educational materials on racial and linguistic diversity, poverty, and inclusion, including writings by Nieto and Ladson-Billings, as well as featuring speakers from each of the two field practicum schools. The data analysis was conducted by using a $2 \times 2$ MANOVA to determine differences in the pre and post condition. As a result of this experience, authors found that cultural diversity awareness increased in several areas, including believing more strongly that students should be identified by ethnic groups, scheduling IEP meetings at the convenience of the parents and including parents in planning student programs, and a lower inclination of referring students for testing if they thought their learning difficulties were due to a cultural or language difference, less accepting of ethnic jokes, and more inclined to rotate the distribution of classroom roles.

## RESULTS

### Demographic Data and Pre-Score Analysis

A one way between subjects ANOVA was conducted to compare the effect of each of the demographic qualifiers collected in the student survey on pre-scores for each subcategory of the CDAI. These qualifiers included the age of the participant, semester the course was taken, program the participant was enrolled in, the perceived diversity of their high school environment, the perceived diversity of their current living environment, previous experience with individuals from other nations, previous training in ME, gender, and race. All demographic qualifiers resulted in nonsignificant p-values, except for the following:

*Semester and Cross-Cultural Communication Pre-Scores*: A one way between subjects ANOVA was conducted to compare the effect of semester on cross-cultural communication pre-score in the semester 1, semester 2, and semester 3 conditions. There was a significant effect of semester on cross-cultural communication pre-scores at the $p < .05$ level for the three conditions ($F[2,82] = 4.430$, $p = 0.015$). Post hoc comparisons using the Tukey HSD test indicated that the mean score for the semester one condition ($M = 9.926$, $SD = 1.184$) was significantly different from the semester three condition ($M = 8.813$, $SD = 1.685$). However, the semester two condition ($M = 9.375$, $SD = 1.218$) did not significantly differ from the semester one and three conditions. These results demonstrate that for some reason, participants in the first semester began the course with higher scores in the cross-cultural communication subgroup.

*Current Living Environment and General Cultural Awareness Pre-Scores*: A one way between subjects ANOVA was conducted to compare the effect of the perception of diversity of living environment on general cultural awareness pre-score in the none, a little, moderate, and a large amount conditions. There was a significant effect of perception of diversity of living environment on general cultural awareness pre-scores at the $p < 0.5$ level for the four conditions ($F[3,82] = 2.710$, $p = 0.051$). Post hoc comparisons using the Tukey HSD test indicated that the mean score for the moderate condition ($M = 19.086$, $SD = 1.962$) was significantly different from the "a little" condition ($M = 17.51$, $SD = 2.095$). However, the "none" condition ($M = 18.750$, $SD = 1.299$) and the "a large amount" conditions ($M = 18.750$, $SD = 2.487$) did not significantly differ from the "a little" and "moderate" conditions. These results demonstrate that participants living in an environment that they perceived as "more diverse" scored higher than those participants living in an environment that they perceived as "less diverse," in the General Cultural Awareness subgroup.

*Previous Experience with Other Nationals and General Cultural Awareness Pre-Scores:* A one way between subjects ANOVA was conducted to compare the effect of experience with individuals from other nations on the general cultural awareness pre-score in the frequent interactions and infrequent interactions conditions. The participant responses were sorted by an initial question "Have you had experiences with someone from another country? (yes/no)." Seventy-two out of eighty-three participants answered that they have had experiences with someone from another country. From this subset of the population, there was a significant effect of frequency of experience on general cultural awareness pre-scores at the $p < .05$ level for the two conditions ($F[1,71] = 5.912$, $p = 0.018$). Post hoc comparisons using the Tukey HSD test indicated that the mean score for the frequent condition ($M = 19.385$, $SD = 1.711$) was significantly different from the infrequent condition ($M = 18.130$, $SD = 2.252$). These results indicate that participants having previous experience with people from other countries were more aware of cultural diversity at the beginning of the course, in the General Cultural Awareness subgroup.

*Gender and Creating a Multicultural Environment Pre-Scores:* A one way between subjects ANOVA was conducted to compare the effect of gender on Creating a Multicultural Environment pre-scores in the male and female conditions. There was a significant effect of gender on creating multicultural environment pre-scores at the $p < .05$ level for the two conditions ($F[1, 82] = 7.608$, $p = 0.007$). Post hoc comparisons using the Tukey HSD test indicated that the mean score for the female condition ($M = 35.805$, $SD = 3.346$) was significantly higher than the male condition ($M = 31.833$, $SD = 3.484$). These results demonstrate that female participants began the course with a higher cultural diversity awareness than males in this subgroup of questions.

## Demographic Data and Post-Score Analysis

A one way between subjects ANOVA was conducted to compare the effect of demographic data collected in this study on the post-score for each subgroup. The results were not statistically significant between any subgroup and any demographic group, demonstrating that while participants may have entered the study with more cultural sensitivity, their demographic group does not have a significant effect on their cultural sensitivity gained during the study.

## Pre-Post Analysis

A paired-samples t-test was conducted to compare CDAI scores for the pre and post conditions. There was a significant difference between the pre and post conditions for some questions, across several subgroups (see tables 3.1–3.4).

From a macro view, when looking at subgroups, three subgroups had items that showed change from the pre and post condition with participants in this study; Creating a Multicultural Environment Using Multicultural Methods and Materials (nine of nine questions), General Cultural Awareness (three of five questions), and the Culturally Diverse Family (two of seven questions). There was no significant difference between pre and post conditions for all questions within two subgroups of the CDAI; Cross-Cultural Communication and Assessment.

Table 3.1 Creating a Multicultural Environment Using Multicultural Methods and Materials: Statistical Analysis of the Creating a Multicultural Environment Using Multicultural Methods and Materials Subgroup, Cultural Diversity Awareness Inventory Instrument

| Question | Pre Mean (SD) | Post Mean (SD) | t-value | p-value |
|---|---|---|---|---|
| The solution to communication problems of certain ethnic groups is the child's own . . . | 1.819 (0.608) | 1.530 (0.669) | 4.425 | *<0.0001 |
| In a society with as many racial groups as the United States, I would expect and accept the use of ethnic . . . | 1.867 (0.852) | 1.639 (0.805) | 2.708 | *0.008 |
| There are times when racial statements should be ignored. | 2.133 (1.091) | 1.855 (1.026) | 3.422 | *0.001 |
| The teaching of ethnic customs and traditions is NOT the responsibility of public school . . . | 2.241 (0.864) | 2.012 (0.789) | 3.208 | *0.002 |
| It is my responsibility to provide opportunities for children to share cultural differences in food . . . | 4.265 (0.700) | 4.506 (0.592) | −3.962 | *0.000 |
| I will make adaptations in programming to accommodate the different cultures as my . . . | 4.060 (0.771) | 4.361 (0.708) | −4.741 | *<0.0001 |
| The displays and frequently used materials within my setting will show at least three different ethnic groups . . . | 3.831 (0.778) | 4.108 (0.781) | −3.885 | *0.000 |
| A regular rotating schedule for job assignments which will include each child within my setting. | 3.928 (0.793) | 4.120 (0.817) | −3.065 | *0.003 |
| One's knowledge of a particular culture should affect one's expectations of the children's performance. | 2.506 (0.992) | 2.241 (1.089) | 2.278 | *0.025 |

*The value is not statistically significant.

## DISCUSSION

This unique approach to teaching utilizing practice-based activities in a foundation course (Ball and Forzani 2009; Breck and Krim 2012) impacted preservice teacher awareness of cultural diversity in a variety of areas. From

**Table 3.2   General Cultural Awareness: Statistical Analysis of the General Cultural Awareness Subgroup, Cultural Diversity Awareness Inventory Instrument**

| Question | Pre Mean (SD) | Post Mean (SD) | t-value | p-value |
|---|---|---|---|---|
| My culture to be different from some of the children I will teach. | 4.193 (0.903) | 4.494 (0.705) | −3.169 | *0.002 |
| It is important to identify immediately the ethnic group of the children I will teach. | 3.530 (0.954) | 3.831 (0.935) | −2.899 | *0.005 |
| I would prefer to work with children and parents whose cultures are similar to mine. | 2.916 (0.965) | 2.759 (0.958) | 1.473 | 0.145 |
| I am uncomfortable in settings with people who exhibit values or beliefs different from my own. | 2.349 (0.847) | 2.133 (0.761) | 2.899 | *0.005 |
| I am sometimes surprised when members of certain ethnic groups contribute to particular . . . | (1.964) (0.818) | 1.867 (0.921) | 1.016 | 0.313 |

these results, we can assess what subgroup areas in the CDAI were impacted by the course curriculum, and which areas were not impacted.

*Creating a Multicultural Environment Using Multicultural Methods and Materials*: The subgroup that shows the most growth as indicated by statistical significance between the pre and post condition after a paired-samples t-test is the Creating a Multicultural Environment Using Multicultural Methods and Materials group. In this group, all nine questions measured an impact on students in this course. The CDAI results for this subgroup of questions illustrate that the curriculum of pen pals and reflection results in teacher candidates becoming more sensitive to their role as a teacher and the power differential that exists within their classroom, understanding that the use of ethnic jokes and phrases are hurtful toward children, understanding the concept of a deficit model and understand that this model perpetuates white hegemony, learning more about the role of a school within the community, about their role as a teacher, the need for a teacher to connect with the community, and that the community is comprised of all of their students and their families, that their classroom community is comprised of all of their students and it is their responsibility to honor all of their students by using identifying visual displays, became more aware of their power in confronting and addressing racial statements, and increased in their understanding of types of adaptations are a way to employ social justice through their instructional approach. While it can be seen as promising that all of the questions in this

**Table 3.3 The Culturally Diverse Family: Statistical Analysis of the Culturally Diverse Family Subgroup, Cultural Diversity Awareness Inventory Instrument**

| Question | Pre Mean (SD) | Post Mean (SD) | t-value | p-value |
|---|---|---|---|---|
| Asking families of diverse cultures how they wish to be referred to at the beginning of our . . . | 2.843 (1.006) | 3.205 (1.124) | −3.27 | *0.002 |
| Other than the required school activities, my interactions with parents should include social . . . | 3.120 (1.052) | 3.325 (1.127) | −1.944 | 0.055 |
| The family's views of school and society should be included in the school's yearly program . . . | 3.723 (.0816) | 3.904 (0.919) | −2.023 | *0.046 |
| It is necessary to include ongoing parent input in program planning. | 4.000 (0.841) | 4.133 (0.745) | −1.586 | 0.117 |
| I sometimes experience frustration when conducting conferences with parents whose . . . | 2.398 (0.811) | 2.530 (0.967) | −1.417 | 0.16 |
| Parents know little about assessing their own children. | 2.386 (0.881) | 2.398 (0.840) | −0.134 | 0.894 |
| Individualized Education Program meetings or program planning should be scheduled for the . . . | 3.928 (0.762) | 4.048 (0.810) | −1.639 | 0.105 |

**Table 3.4 Cross-Cultural Communication: Statistical Analysis of the Cross-Cultural Communication Subgroup, Cultural Diversity Awareness Inventory Instrument**

| Question | Pre Mean (SD) | Post Mean (SD) | t-value | p-value |
|---|---|---|---|---|
| I would be uncomfortable in settings with people who speak nonstandard English. | 2.916 (1.095) | 2.747 (1.103) | 1.600 | 0.113 |
| English should be taught as a second language to non-English speaking children as a regular . . . | 3.867 (0.866) | 4.000 (0.749) | −1.372 | 0.174 |
| When correcting a child's spoken language, one should role model without any further . . . | 2.687 (0.936) | 2.566 (1.014) | 1.165 | 0.247 |
| That there are times when the use of nonstandard English should be ignored. | 2.783 (0.925) | 2.940 (0.929) | −1.886 | 0.063 |

subsection showed a statistically significant and positive change from the pre and post conditions, viewed through another lens, such as that of simulated tolerance, the phenomena discussed earlier, all of these questions can be seen as a task to be *done* within the classroom, and do not represent a preservice teacher's personal preference or behavior outside of the classroom.

*General Cultural Awareness:* The next subgroup to be impacted by this course curriculum is the General Cultural Awareness subgroup, in which three of five questions showed statistical significance between the pre and post condition. Teacher candidates in this study became more aware of the current demographics of K-12 students and that this range of demographics is not aligned with the demographic representation of K-12 teachers, understanding a student's ethnicity is important in better understanding the individual child, and more comfortable through the pen pal experience, after having conversations with peers who exhibited values and beliefs different from their own.

The questions that did not show statistical significance between the pre and post conditions are: "I would prefer to work with children and parents whose cultures are similar to mine," and "I am sometimes surprised when members of certain ethnic groups contribute to particular school programs, (e.g. bilingual students on the debate team or Black students in the orchestra)." Our rationale for the results for the "preference" question within this subgroup is similar to Larke's findings in 1990, when she stated, "The degree of sensitivity varies greatly depending upon how the issue is viewed. For example, when asked questions that posed a conflict of values or not wanting to state "true" feeling, neutral answers were recorded" (27). The scores of the "preference" question are close to neutral and can be explained by Larke's theory. The scores of the "surprise" question are not neutral but show no statistical significance from the pre to the post condition, however, in tandem, the "preference" and "surprise" questions have to do with one's personal and intimate thoughts and feelings. Contrastingly, the three questions within this subsection for which the scores were statistically significant between the pre and post conditions all have to do with interpersonal interactions with others in the school setting, again pointing toward simulated tolerance.

*The Culturally Diverse Family:* The last subgroup to show growth as measured by the CDAI is the Culturally Diverse Family subgroup, in which two of seven questions showed statistical significant difference between the pre and post condition. Results suggest that teacher candidates in this study became more aware of the perspective of diverse cultures, and that the person's choice of how they should be referred to should be respected and upheld, and learned more about the role of a school within the community.

The questions that did not show statistical significance in scores from the pre to the post condition are: "Other than the required school activities, my interactions with parents should include social events, meeting in public places (e.g. shopping centers), or telephone conversations." Here, the pre- and post-scores are close to neutral, and some activities suggested by this question imply work on the teacher's part to make special effort outside of the designated school day. The next question, "It is necessary to include on-going parent input in program planning" shows scores are not significant, and close to "strongly agree." Authors are satisfied with this response, even though it is not significant, as it seems to be aligned with cultural diversity awareness from the pre CDAI assessment. The next question, "I sometimes experience frustration when conducting conferences with parents whose culture is different from my own" shows scores that are close to neutral, question asks about personal thoughts and feelings. "Parents know little about assessing their own children" shows scores are close to neutral, question asks about personal thoughts and feelings. The last question, "Individualized Education Program meetings or program planning should be scheduled for the convenience of the parents" shows scores are not close to neutral, and authors are satisfied with this outcome, as it seems to be aligned with cultural diversity awareness in this area from the pre CDAI assessment. Again, student responses to questions within subgroups can be explained by Larke's 1990 findings of neutral scores representing responses to questions as posing a conflict of values or indicating that students did not want to state true feelings; and the "public" or "private" nature of the questions point to a simulated tolerance documented in work conducted by Evans-Winters and Hoff in 2011. In contrast, authors see a different trend when examining the subgroup areas that were not shown to be statistically significant in total; that of Cross-Cultural Communication and Assessment (see table 3.5).

Table 3.5 Assessment: Statistical Analysis of the Assessment Subgroup, Cultural Diversity Awareness Inventory Instrument

| Question | Pre Mean (SD) | Post Mean (SD) | t-value | p-value |
| --- | --- | --- | --- | --- |
| A child should be referred for testing if learning difficulties appear to be due to cultural . . . | 3.048 (1.047) | 2.916 (1.150) | 1.351 | 0.181 |
| Adaptations in standardized assessments to be questionable since they alter reliability and . . . | 3.108 (0.897) | 3.133 (1.113) | −0.253 | 0.801 |
| Translating a standardized achievement or intelligence test to the child's dominant . . . | 2.386 (1.102) | 2.253 (1.167) | 1.394 | 0.167 |

*Cross-Cultural Communication:* Almost all of the questions in this subgroup resulted in pre- and post-scores that are close to neutral, again indicating that these questions may have posed a conflict of values or implied that students did not want to state their true feelings. It is reassuring that students answered the "second language" question in a manner that aligns with understanding cultural diversity and that it is the right of non-English speaking children to receive instruction in English as a second language. In addition, authors believe that a lack of statistical significance in the pre- and post-scores for the cross-cultural communication subgroup indicate something that points to the nature of our schooling system; the myth that "academics" should look a certain way. Students should sit still in their chairs and desks, work quietly, move from one classroom to another at the prompting of a bell, and raise their hands to speak. Along with these criteria, the writing that is considered "academic" should be free of contractions and use "proper English" language. Nonstandard language should always be corrected. The perpetuating of this myth has very troubling consequences. The language that is used by underserved populations should be honored and respected as its own dialect, and students should not be admonished or corrected when not using "proper academic English." Authors purport that our preservice students that were surveyed in these areas still hold on to this myth as truth. This is disappointing, as communication cannot occur between individuals when one of the individuals refuses to listen to the other until they say their thoughts in a "proper" way. Communication in this situation is halted. In contrast, when individuals who are communicating focus on the intention of the statements, rather than the grammar with which the thoughts are communicated, cross-cultural communication can flourish. When communication takes place across cultures, change, understanding, meaningful interactions, and compassion for the "other" can take place. Without cross-cultural communication, all is lost. These results indicate that our students are uncomfortable in situations that require cross-cultural communication, and in future courses, we need to support and instruct them on having these conversations by modeling and additional high-impact activities. Authors feel that components could be added to courses specifically devoted to literacy that would address these areas and provide a setting in which students can talk openly and honestly about their concerns and questions.

*Assessment:* Participant scores for all three questions; "A child should be referred for testing if learning difficulties appear to be due to cultural differences and/or language," "Adaptations in standardized assessments to be questionable since they alter reliability and validity," and "Translating a standardized achievement or intelligence test to the child's dominant language gives the child an added advantage and does not allow for peer comparison" did not show statistical significance, and hover around the neutral category, indicating a conflict of values or unwillingness to state a "true" feeling, as claimed by Larke (1990). The scenarios described by these items, if addressed appropriately, would allow fair testing for all students. Because our participants scored these items as they did, authors purport that not only may there be a conflict of values, or an unwillingness to state a true feeling, but that privilege is at play here. Academic standardized testing has long been known to be biased toward white students (Jaschik 2010; Rosales 2018), and answering these questions appropriately (A child should *not* be referred for testing if learning difficulties appear to be due to cultural differences and/or language; Adaptations in standardized assessments are not questionable, but fair, and translating a standardized achievement or intelligence test to the child's dominant language does *not* give the child an added advantage, but levels the playing field) would allow access for underserved populations to achieve to their full ability. Authors feel that components could be added to courses specifically devoted to assessment that would address these areas and provide a setting in which students can talk openly and honestly about their concerns and questions.

While we have seen that there are areas in which preservice teachers in this course shift their cultural diversity awareness in some areas, we have also seen that there are areas in which they do not significantly shift their awareness. The findings further reinforce the research that illustrates that one course is not enough to make a significant difference.

## RECOMMENDATIONS FOR FURTHER STUDY

The prominent studies featured above that utilized the CDAI instrument to study their students illustrate three important points: (1) most teacher education students are white and female. (2) CDAI scores from 1990 to 2020 can be used to conduct a longitudinal study of types that creates a profile across time of preservice attitudes and beliefs, and we call for research to address this need. (3) Not only does the preservice teacher population need to be made more diverse, but it is inherent to study students of color in addition to white students. In each of the highlighted studies, the number of students of color is not large enough to conduct a statistical analysis between and within groups. Until this number of preservice students is increased, there is a lack of information teacher educators and researchers will have in relationship to what works best for students of color in a course on diversity. Sadly, this is not a phenomena that is specific to education. In 2019, Krim et al.'s review of science research experiences noted just that, stating,

> We join others in reiterating the call for more studies that 1) purposefully target a diverse participant sample and 2) rigorously collect, analyze, and report data

that reflect outcomes that may be unique for women and participants of color. Such studies will lead to increasingly better understanding of new approaches to undergraduate and teacher course and programs that result in enhanced representation in STEM fields. *If we are to make strides toward equity and diversity in STEM fields, researchers and program developers alike need to intentionally develop programs that not only attract and facilitate diverse participation, but also consider specific attention toward data collection, analysis, and reporting that reflects this goal.* (10)

Lortie's "apprenticeship of observation" illustrates that while most preservice teachers have had a significant amount of time observing a teacher (as a student), they have very little understanding of the transformational work (Howard 2006) that must be done, or the "behind the scenes" administrivia. However, preservice teachers who have a family member or close friend who was a teacher have quite a different view of what teachers actually do. In further studies, authors feel it would be interesting to examine the scores of preservice teachers who fell into each of these categories (teacher as family or friend/no teacher as family or friend) to understand if one group scored significantly different in the pre and post conditions.

Lastly, authors call on future researchers to examine the phenomena of simulated tolerance, and research or develop processes by which this behavior can be unpacked, allowing a re-education for white preservice teachers. It has been stated time and time again that white teachers need to do the work to examine their own Whiteness. These two concepts go hand in hand. It is time for a new paradigm in education, one which will truly include and serve all students. From national policies, to reliance on standardized testing, to one teacher's classroom in mid-America, the time has come to cause change.

*Chapter 4*

# Critical Race Theory

Critical Race Theory (CRT) is a theoretical framework arising out of a movement undertaken by scholars and activists which highlights the connections between race, racism, and power (Delagado and Stefancic, 2001). These scholars and activists have given a credible voice to the people holding marginalized identities. CRT has a foundation in critical legal studies and radical feminism, holding space among academics in a new approach to critical analysis (Delgado and Stefancic, 2001). Critical Legal Studies (CLS) challenges traditional legal scholarship to a form of law that looks at individuals and groups within social, political, and cultural contexts, and CRT honors these power imbalances between opposing parties. Scholars within CLS expose the inconsistencies, both internal and external, of the law that supports America's present class-based, race-based, and gender-based social structure. CLS confronts traditional legal dogma that portrays American society as a meritocracy but ignores the racism embedded within its institutions and structures (Delagado and Stefancic, 2001). The framework of CRT has evolved to include education, political science, and ethnic studies. In contrast to most academic discipline studies, CRT honors the activist voice. CRT focuses on two distinct features: The first feature acknowledges that racism is normal. It is not a human phenomenon that occurs in a vacuum or the exception to behavioral norms. Racism is normalized in American culture, and discrimination and prejudicial statements are commonly experienced by people with marginalized identities. The second feature acknowledges that the power dynamic of white over color is intentional. When adherence to the power dynamic is present, financial and material benefits are positioned for people who identify as white. CRT claims that the following universal truths apply to institutional structures within US society: (1) race and racism are central, endemic, permanent, and essential in defining and explaining how US society functions; (2) dominant ideologies and claims of race neutrality, objectivity, meritocracy, color blindness, and equal opportunity must be challenged; (3) progression is activist in nature and propagates a commitment to social justice; (4) the experiences and voices of the marginalized and oppressed must be made central; and (5) it is necessary to view scope and function in an interdisciplinary manner (Delgado Bernal 2002; Delgado and Stefancic 2001; Solorzano and Yosso 2002).

## INTEREST CONVERGENCE

Interest convergence appears in three places within teacher preparation programs across colleges and universities, both public and private, nationwide; (1) the racial composition of teacher education faculty is mostly white, (2) the context of multicultural courses are a structure of Eurocentric White-dominant P-12 curricula which is a celebration of differences instead of systemic inequalities, (3) the relationship of teacher education and the university is to maintain the production of large numbers of white teacher candidates. These teacher preparation programs serve large numbers of students in relatively low-cost programs generating revenue and provide support to other programs within the university by providing graduates career paths, that is, English and History Bachelor's Degrees (Sleeter 2017).

## INTERSECTIONALITY

In more recent developments, CRT scholars have embedded the concept of intersectionality into their scholarship. While the concept of intersectionality is alone worthy of its own book, Critical scholars of law and other social sciences have highlighted the complexities of overlapping identities that may or may not be conflicting (Delagado and Stefancic, 2001). For example, the white female with a Latina ethnicity, who may also identify as an atheist and lesbian and is part of the poor working-class has multiple identities that at times conflict within herself and with society. Atheism is typically an outlier in Latin cultures that are predominately Latin Roman Catholic. Within her family, lesbianism and atheism would be in conflict with the predominant cultural expectations of the religious doctrine her family and community follow. Because CRT asserts that class and gender cannot be divorced from the topic of race (Crenshaw, 1989), this intersectionality allows for the strategic ignoring of race which in turn supports the mechanism that facilitates whiteness in teacher education, even when topics of class and gender are included (Matias, Montoya and Nishi, 2016). If we, as the educational community, focus on poverty and sexism, race can be a topic that is not fully addressed when discussing curriculum, policy, or power dynamics within the classroom. When we continue to collapse ideas of race with other demographic measures, the structures that support a white supremacist ideology remain dominant in public education. "Poverty," "urban," and "ghetto" become the words we use to address disparities between student outcomes without ever having to address race, although each of these terms has been used to be synonymous with Black and Brown folk in white spaces. Teacher preparation programs have highlighted academic research around poverty to classify Black and Brown children without having to address race (Ladson-Billings, 2009).

Claims of neutrality, color blindness, and meritocracy uphold the dominant ideologies. Whiteness claims that individual successes are achieved within a system of competitive individualism, to talent and effort. CRT holds these claims of neutrality and color blindness as masks that conceal white privilege and power (Sleeter 2017).

## GIVING VOICE TO THE VOICELESS: VOICE OF COLOR

In addition to intersectionality, CRT scholars have begun to acknowledge the "voice of color" (Delagado and Stefancic, 2001, 9). Experiential knowledge is honored within CRT and values counter stories, believing that those who are victims of racism understand it best, rather than the perpetrators of systemic white supremacy (Sleeter 2017). This acknowledgment adds a presumed credibility to speak to race and racism as a narrative, created by individual experiences that often lead to a larger understanding of institutional racism. An example of this is the "driving while Black phenomenon." In the 1990s, this societal phenomenon gained momentum in mainstream circles as people of color began telling their stories of being pulled over by law enforcement for such contrived or meaningless purposes as driving in the wrong area of town, or that their car was suspicious "in this neighborhood." These narratives illustrate racialized and classist viewpoints of which "type" of people belong in white spaces. People of color, especially Black males, began to discuss these experiences with police to larger audiences in contrast to the normalized tales told only to their innermost circles. As their stories spread, more Black males began to talk about these experiences, and an institutionalized policy of discrimination toward Black male drivers within the law enforcement system was exposed. This outcome of Black men sharing experiences of "driving while Black" is just one example of the power that exists when credibility is given to the voice of color. The #MeToo movement, #BlackLivesMatter movement, and #TakeAKnee movement are all examples of activism that began by people of color and other marginalized identities. When marginalized people began to discuss their individual experiences of discrimination as they complete everyday tasks within society (i.e., driving, working, shopping, and socializing), an organic formation of a collective awareness began. It became undeniably clear that these daily experiences are not individual incidents of racism, sexism, xenophobia, classism, and others, but rather an institutionalized practice within society.

One may think that these movements, this acknowledgment, given to the voice of color, is evidence that the United States has made progress in its work on race, moving from acknowledging base level white supremacist ideology to unpacking the racialized politics within society and more extremist hate groups. However, CRT scholars argue that mainstream political parties, the education system, and other functioning governmental agencies are actively maintaining and extending the power dynamic that white people have on "Western" capitalist societies (Gillborn, 2005). CRT scholars argue for an alternate interpretation of the role of educational policy. CRT's perspective on race and education views policy as, at best, acting to preserve the status quo and defend the state of white supremacy as "normal," rejecting claims of progress toward equity and social justice in public education.

## WITHIN EDUCATION

CRT gives voice to the voiceless in educational settings in a number of ways. The impact of the landmark Brown V. Board of Education decision created "equal opportunity" for Black students within public education spaces (Ladson-Billings, 2009). However, the notion of offering sameness in 1955 to white and Black students did not address past inequities. As a result, today's Black students are seen as having to catch up to their white peers without any applicable practices to address decades of segregated school and over 200 years of prohibiting Black children from participating in formal education settings (Ladson-Billing, 2009). Likewise, throughout this time, any child who did not hold white, male, Christian, heterosexual, or middle-class identity also experienced past inequities in public education spaces. For example, females were educationally tracked into programs for clerical, secretarial, nursing, and education work until they were married. Once married, females were expected to stay at home with the children and support their husband's careers, but if they attended school, they again were tracked into programs consisting of courses in cooking, sewing, etiquette, and managing a home. For decades, women were institutionally forced into this program of study. Furthermore, in today's current public education spaces, we see a disparity in the enrollment of females in the STEM disciplines. There are now active efforts to recruit and retain women into these disciplines in an attempt to address past inequities by simply allowing females access to these types of courses, or even blocking their way by encouraging them to take on another, "more suitable," career path.

CRT views curriculum and teacher practices within public education as highly problematic. When analyzing an official school curriculum through a CRT lens, it is clear that the dominant culture emolument is designed to uphold a white supremacist ideology (Ladson-Billings, 2009). This curriculum is strategic in muting the voices of the marginalized in comparison to the white voices. History and societal events are presented in the binary of winners and losers. For example, scientists and mathematicians are given credit for their work and theorems without the acknowledgment of the contributions of others that were vital to the completion of their work. Watson and Crick are a classic example of this phenomenon; two men received credit for their discovery of DNA, and this discovery is a keystone understanding upon which the science discipline is based. However, Rosalind Franklin was the first person to capture images of the DNA helix, providing the data that Watson and Crick used to build their structure. When school curricula and teachers fail to give voice or acknowledgment to women who contributed (and in this case originated) scientific work, the white supremacist curricula is supported and held firmly in place.

CRT purports that current instructional strategies presume that Black and Brown children are deficient to their white peers. In teacher education programs, merit and credibility are given to instructional strategies that support teacher candidates in "handling" or "dealing with" "at-risk" students. These terms are loaded in that they address racial differences in student outcomes by focusing on the strategy rather than the racism. The language of instructional practice and traditional pedagogy is framed to focus on the deficiency of the student and the necessary remediation (Ladson-Billing, 2009). Because of this language within educational theory and practice, CRT examines the use of language within educational theory and practice, providing a critical analysis of the fundamental nature of white supremacy in education (Matias, Montoya and Nishi, 2016).

## WHY TEACHER PREPARATION

Teacher preparation programs are the best place to study and understand the emotionality of Whiteness because it is an institutionally protected process that continually produces almost 90 percent of the teaching force. There is a critical and urgent need to impact teacher preparation programs because the demographics of teachers and their accompanying belief systems are so severely misaligned with the demographics of the students they teach. For an excellent primer on white emotionality, we recommend *The Twin Tales of Whiteness: Exploring the Emotional Rollercoaster of Teaching and Learning about whiteness* (Matias, Henry, and Darland 2017). Teacher preparation programs can only be impacted in their approach to inclusivity through a CRT lens. One key factor that must be considered is the emotionality of Whiteness and its correlation with how race is blocked inside teacher education (Matias, Montoya and Nishi 2016). Stovall corroborated this by asserting that CRT and social justice are constants that require "the recognition of the interplay of race and class" in education and justice (2006, 257).

> *When applied to teacher education, CRT deconstructs how race manifests itself in ideologies, epistemologies, and practices that undergird curricula, pedagogical instruction, and educational thought. (Matias, Montoya and Nishi, 2016, 3)*

Critical Whiteness studies support CRT's analysis of race and process of understanding of how white supremacy is experienced by people of color, so that it may be dismantled. Critical Whiteness studies demonstrate how white people are normalized and, therefore, participants in their own supremacy (Matias, Montoya and Nishi, 2016).

The authors' application of the CRT lens to their work and research brings attention to Whiteness as it permeates the knowledge, pedagogies, and ideologies within the institution of public education. Essentially, this caters to the emotionality of Whiteness embedded in teacher preparation programs. The authors access CRT theoretical framework as they analyze data that is collected in teacher preparation programs. The goals of CRT in education vary widely among scholars, but each reflects the same types of variation found in the conceptualizations of CRT (Thankdeka, 2013). The conceptualization of CRT noted in the universal truths reported above guides the authors' analysis of the students' work in these teacher preparation programs. The links between CRT and social justice are often misinterpreted, as scholarship that seeks equity and exposes inequity through academic discourse through the CRT lens is only one part of education. As the field of education has evolved, social justice and CRT have come to mean enactments of a practice, rather than the scholarship itself (Thankdeka, 2013). Acknowledging this practice within the teacher education programs is essential to ensuring that the teacher candidate has the knowledge and tools with which to create classroom environments that are inclusive to all children.

> Pre-service teachers internalized notions of race and white racial superiority is of concern to critical race scholars and feminist in education (Henry 1993). CRT provides a point of departure from narratives of innocence that serve to

protect institutional liberalism in education programs. Scholars in education point out the relevancy of CRT to educational policy, curriculum, assessment, and discourse.

(Evans-Winters, Venus and Pamela Twyman Hoff, 2011, 466)

The overall message underlying white students' resistance to a culturally responsive pedagogy and critical race analysis is that they have to engage in conversations of race, class, and gender difference and equity (Evans-Winters and Hoff, 2011). Refusing to participate in such discourse is one example of white students invoking their racial power to avoid feelings of uncomfortability. White faculty members in teacher education programs can access language like "poverty," "ghetto," "urban," and other loaded words to calm the emotional Whiteness in the room and maintain engagement levels.

When the stability of this system is threatened by calls for change, the interests of the white majority coincide with the protests of the marginalized group. Some concessions may be granted, but the stability of the systems remains unchanged. The contradiction between discourse and practice has been given a concession then, and the dominant policy does not need to actually change to offer equitable outcomes (Gillborn, 2013). The consideration of three CRT concepts: interest convergence, contradiction-closing cases, and interest divergence provide the vital tools for CRT analysis of education policy, that is, a perspective that thoroughly confronts the long-established view of policy as a cumulative process moving toward justice and inclusion of all students. CRT proclaims policy as an essential apparatus in the continuous struggle for racial justice against an establishment of white supremacy (Gillborn, 2013). CRT perceives policy not as a process that is shaped by the interests of the dominant white population but as a vehicle of social justice that is part of a mechanism that achieves genuine progress won through political protest but has it's apparent gains quickly cut back via policy to maintain status quo (Gillborn, 2013). The *interest convergence* principle in CRT is essential to understanding that it does not confront a logical and balanced compromise between marginalized groups and white power holders, instead where change is achieved through meer force of reason and logic (Gillborn, 2013). Interest convergence is more about an intersectional analysis of race and class interests. It views whites holding lower-class status and minimized social collateral as a kind of intermediator that protects the interest of upper-class whites with greater social capital, especially when disputed by high-profile race equality or civil rights campaigns (Gillmore, 2013). Interest convergence can serve as a beneficial analytical tool to deconstruct policy and practice in teacher education and to address the lack of the under-presumption of race in public education. Interest convergence is founded in perspectives that develop the theory and practice of teacher education as a pre-arranged design by the relationship of race that dominates in the larger culture (Milner, Pearman III, and McGhee, 2013). Both interest convergence and divergence together explain policy as a continuous crusade to secure privilege and control to the dominant white interests. *Interest divergence* is defined as white power holders maintaining their privilege and racial inequity in social structures and political institutions. The perspective of interest divergence as a powerful explanatory device in deconstructing how white supremacy is protected and empowered through the construction and manipulation of the apparent interest divergence between racial groups (Gillborn, 2013). Public education demonstrates the interest convergence and interest divergence through a curriculum of white dominance and the relentless testing of students on exams standardized to white, male, middle-class, Christian culture. It is important for those of us preparing teacher candidates to name the existence of race in public education. The teacher candidates must understand the foundational tools and the definitive language and concepts that can be used to study, analyze, discuss, explain, and ultimately name these realities for people of color that may contribute to the white-dominant policy, research, and theory that dictate teacher education policy and practices (Milner, Pearman III, and McGhee, 2013). *Contradiction-Closing Cases* refer to transformations in policy that appear to confront an overt injustice. Instead, they remove the conflict between a clear injustice and the official discourse of equality and fairness (Gillborn, 2013). Racial indifference and the perception of color blindness infuse mainstream teacher education programs, research, policy, and practice (Milner, Pearman III, and McGhee, 2013). A movement within teacher education to address this indifference to race and color-blind perspective is growing and gaining momentum. Current practices of adding people of color as faculty into teacher preparation programs and the inclusion of culturally responsive pedagogy, restorative practices, and instructional interventions for academics and behavior are not addressing the white supremacist mentality or the white supremacist curriculum that was taught in K-12 settings of the teacher candidate. CRT scholars perceive color blindness as the problem, not the solution. The questionable appearance of color blindness can be seen in the segregation experienced by both students and teachers (Anderson and Cross, 2013). The idea of color blindness as quality teaching declines to report the ways in which race impacts education and upholds the Whiteness of teacher education. As an example, in their analysis of advertising for Teach for America (TFA), Milner and Howard (2013) point out that the notion of seeking the "best and the brightest" teacher candidates has led TFA to target elite institutions in which enrollment of students of color is disproportionately low (Sleeter, 2017). While TFA claims to provide diversity training and to have an inclusive approach (http://www.hssu.edu/deptdocs/17/HBCU.OP.Color.pdf), upon closer examination of this approach, seen through the lens of participants of color, Lapayese, Aldana, and Lara (2014) found that the curriculum and instruction provided to participants are focused on the growth and knowledge of white teachers, and does little to support teachers of color; its overall efforts could be described as "superficial" at best. White (2016) finds TFA's two-pronged approach of serving as an alternative certification program and an influential policy actor to be paradoxical. It seems as though this self-proclaimed leadership model for education reform is quite insidious in nature, doing more to damage communities of color and displace new teachers of color, perpetuating (if not worsening) the status quo.

Teacher education faculty must be explicit in the instruction of exposing and challenging the racists policies and practices within teacher education and public schools. Recommended by Milner et al., four areas teacher education programs must address include curriculum and instructional practices, racial backgrounds of teacher educators, the varied routes into teaching (i.e., Teach for America), and school-university partnerships that expose how race maneuvers within each area and elevates the extent to which each of these areas erode the success of people of color (2013). Embracing a CRT lens when developing courses and deciding on the content within those courses, teacher education faculty can expose these inequities within public education as a revolutionary act of change. A CRT lens on teacher education is similar to applying a new paradigm that provides an alternate perception of teacher preparation into a sociopolitical and sociocultural context in which schools continue to fail students of color in public education, especially in the poor and marginalized communities. CRT offers a pathway to focus on some of the predictable practices (i.e., at-risk labels, classroom management, and white-dominant curriculum) of teacher education that operate to maintain the failing urban school as an oppressive institution (Anderson and Cross, 2013).

## RETRAINING TEACHERS TO CRITICALLY ANALYZE CURRICULA AND INSTRUCTION THROUGH THE LENS OF THE MARGINALIZED

America has always prided itself on the existence of two myths; that of the "melting pot," and that of the "American dream." America is a place where anyone can become rich, famous, or access privileges in society through hard work and determination. This myth of meritocracy within America's class system is believed today with as much conviction as when the country was born; it is the core of the American culture. For most children attending K-12 public schools, meritocracy is taught as explicitly as content. However, the truth of the class system in America is that there has always been a power dynamic between the races and social classes from the arrival of the first slave ship in 1605, evident in the "No Irish Need Apply" storefront signs during the industrial revolution, in the Japanese internment camps of the Second World War and today's town hall chants to "Build the Wall." Those of us in teacher education have a responsibility to strategically undo this teaching. Our re-teaching must focus on an understanding of the existence of collective white dominance through social policy, governing, and legislation, acknowledgment of the challenges people with marginalized identities face when confronting white dominance, and building teacher candidates' skills in how to represent these truths within K-12 classrooms. It is imperative that today's teachers understand this dynamic and how it plays out in the classroom, community, and societal institutions, and that they model this understanding in their teaching. It is vital to the future that teacher preparation programs strategically teach CRT theoretical framework as a lens with which to analyze current public school curriculum. For example, in a foundational education course, teacher candidates should come away with an understanding of the history of CLS and its evolution to CRT which is a part of a variety of includes disciplines that access this framework to achieve strategic planning goals. It is important for administrators of teacher education programs to be aware of and question how white interests are being protected through additive steps such as hiring a professor of color, adding a diversity course, or offering a one-shot class or programming event aimed at addressing inequities. The CRT principle of interest convergence demonstrates how the racial composition of teacher education faculty, the content of teacher education curricula, and the relationships between teacher education and the rest of the university tend to maintain the status quo (Sleeter, 2017).

The essential piece to teacher education programs is to give voice to the historically voiceless. Within the myth of meritocracy, the dominant rhetoric attributes people's widely varied levels of success to talent and effort and explains away racial inequities with claims of poor performance while at the same time holding people of color to the same standards and ignoring the deep-rooted effects of historical racism that is institutionalized into social structures. In contrast, CRT holds that claims of neutrality and color-blindness mask white privilege and power (Sleeter, 2017). The oppressor/colonizer curriculum that upholds white supremacy in public education is saturated with these principles of meritocracy. For example, Christopher Columbus is presented as a great conqueror and explorer, extolling his accomplishments in a vacuum of his own will, determination, and talents. However, when one digs deeper into his story, they discover that he was in debt to his home country of Italy and condemned as a con artist. He sought the resources of Spain to pay off Italy and save himself from debtor's prison. He made a deal with the Queen of Spain with promises of slaves, spices, and other natural resources from India in order to have his debts to Italy paid. This transactional relationship resulted in his title of the "Architect of Genocide." Evidenced by his ship's manifest, we now know that Columbus was an inept explorer who was lost at sea, and due to his own miscalculation, only made it to the Caribbean. Once arriving, he committed genocide and other horrendous acts to keep himself from prison (Zinn, 1980). Meritocracy is demonstrated in a win-lose scenario where Columbus is honored as a great man, being lost is a facade for discovery, and conquering of Indigenous peoples is camouflaged as an act of progress. From a binary perspective, colonization and oppression of native peoples is a win for Europe in the sense that historical events or persons maintain the status quo of a white supremacist ideology in a white-dominant world. Imagine the type of socially just discourse that would be available if we told the truth about Columbus and gave voice to the experience of the Arawak people upon Columbus "discovering" their land. Accessing the CRT tools of study, analysis, discourse, and ultimately naming existing or past inequities committed upon people with marginalized identities allows a broader perspective of how systemic inequities like racism, sexism, heteronormativity, classism, and xenophobia can exist in our governmental institutions and societal structures, such as public education.

In social studies and history curricula, one finds limited references to US racial and ethnic minorities, and none to US Latinos. In most areas of the United States, teachers receive certification in the discipline of social studies without any content knowledge from ethnic studies. In addition, Kohli reported that teacher candidates with a degree in ethnic studies found it difficult to pass certification requirements (2013). These certification requirements maintain a Eurocentric focus in the curriculum, which discourages prospective teacher candidates of color (Sleeter, 2017). In addition, it is a blatantly inaccurate view of the experience of American citizens. CRT helps to expose various ways in which teacher education that claims a color-blind status in fact serves Whiteness in teacher education. State policies of certification, tests to enter and/or exit teacher education, and the program of study that counts on full-time students on a university campus all maintain Whiteness (Sleeter, 2017). If teacher candidates experience their content areas and pedagogical courses through a CRT lens, the paradigm around curriculum shifts from one of a winner-loser binary to one which views policies and practices as securing white dominance and marginalizing all other identities.

Retraining teachers in this way to critically analyze curricula through the lens of the marginalized is the crux of social justice work. In 2018, the ACLU reported that for the first time in educational history the percentage of nonwhite students has reached 50 percent (ACLU, 2018). This is a turning point for public education and teacher programs. Those of us in teacher education must acknowledge the universal truths around learning—that it requires student engagement, application to real-world experiences, and representation.

Teaching from a Eurocentric curricula and a white-dominant ideology causes students with marginalized identities to disengage from content, find no application to their real-life experiences, and zero representation of their own cultures in the curricula.

*Chapter 5*

# What Are the Steps to Interrupting the Cycle?

## RECOMMENDATIONS FOR TEACHER EDUCATION PROGRAMS AND FACULTY

Regarding preservice programming, the authors believe that this pivotal topic must not only be addressed within one class taken by teacher candidates. There must be an infusion of Social Justice and Culturally Responsive Teaching (CRT) into the entire curriculum. But first, the old curriculum must be examined for falsehoods, cover-ups, and outright lies told by publishers and editors to whitewash our country's sordid history. "From the North to the South, corporate curriculum lies to our students, conceals pain and injustice, masks racism, and demeans our Black students" (Watson, Hagopian, and Au, 2018). These representations of history which place white men on a pedestal, downplay historical errors, and disregard the existence of people of color and their contributions to our history must be eradicated from the curriculum altogether. It goes without saying that the majority of curricula available are dominated by the economy and politics of California and Texas, so searching out appropriate texts that will address social justice in the classroom will be necessary; these types of curricula most likely will not be located with major publishers. Joel Spring's American Education states, "Textbooks are a traditional means of instilling political values . . . textbook content is highly politicized with many conflicts over what values should appear on their pages. These controversies are highlighted by the state adoption policies in California and Texas and pressures on textbook publishers by special-interest groups" (p.18). Spring goes on to purport that the reason why history textbooks have "historically" seemed so bland is that this is a result of publishers wishing to avoid controversy. Programs and individuals interested in making real change will have to seek out culturally appropriate texts and train their faculty to teach from them, as difficult questions may arise that they will be called to answer to and for.

While a program director is required to align curriculum with state standards, the common trend is to rely on national standards, such as Common Core (http://www.corestandards.org), or Early Learning Standards (https://www.naeyc.org), as well as state standards that mirror national pedagogical content standards. However, while these standards may imply the use of or even dabble in culturally responsive pedagogy, they do not take a social justice approach, and although they have taglines such as "Preparing America's Students for Success," "Creating the Conditions for Success," these nationally based standards do not examine the systemic policies that keep white supremacy in place. Periodically, states will address areas of need with required standards such as Social Emotional Learning Standards (K-12 Learning Goals for SEL, 2018) and Diversity and Inclusion Standards.

In an article written in 2004, Burbach and Noissey completed a critical review of the standards listed in the Interstate Teacher Assessment Supports Consortium (INTASC), National Council for Accreditation of Teacher Education (NCATE), and National Board for Professional Teacher Standards (NBPTS) and found that these standards use language around inclusion in equity, however, failed to offer support in unpacking the meaning. These federal standards need to be more explicit in the link between teaching for diversity and critical equity practice and emphasize a focus on self-reflection of implicit biases educators hold (Burbach and Nassoiy, 2004). Since 2004, the Federal Department of Education reports that most states are moving toward these standards through federal programs such as; Title I, Every Student Succeeds Act, Individuals with Disabilities Education Act, and many others under the Federal Equity and Excellence Commission (https://www.ed.gov/equity). In 2018, the State of Illinois created a team of educators, administrators, teacher preparation program professors, students, and board members to create licensing and certification standards for teachers. This task force was comprised of Diverse and Learner Ready Teachers (DLRT), who were tasked with the construction of standards for culturally relevant teaching (https://www.isbe.net/dlrt).

Regarding the disposition of teacher candidates, it is clear to the authors that while free speech is supported within the classroom, hate speech is not. Providing a space to create this distinction for teacher candidates is crucial. In addition, teacher educators delivering courses that teach social justice and anti-racism, along with culturally responsive pedagogy, must initially set up the parameters and intention for the classroom. For example, in the syllabus and introduction to the class, as well as delivering frequent reminders throughout the semester. The teacher educator must address what the course will accomplish, and why it is being taught. Additionally, addressing the manner in which the course is taught will support all students in learning. Throughout the semester students will not just be asked to be reflective, as addressed in study presented in chapter 3, they will be confronted with their bias and their privilege, and be exposed to others' biases and perspectives in a new light. These activities take place through the coursework and the rigor of the faculty member themselves. Appendix II provides a sample course description of one author's classroom.

The entire program needs to adopt and implement the use of standards frameworks such as Social Justice Standards: the Teaching Tolerance Antibias Framework (2016), which provides anchor standards, grade level outcomes, and antibias scenarios for age ranges K-2, 3–5, 6–8, and 9–12. These standards are organized around four anchor standards and domains, that include identity, diversity, justice, and action. Once these standards are adopted, they must be addressed in every single class in the program. The Framework "Teaching for Black Lives" along with others from the Rethinking Schools Publishing in Milwaukee, Wisconsin, provides a curricular perspective that is forward-gazing, timely, and necessary for the curriculum of today.

Adopting and being trained to implement a curriculum based upon social justice and anti-racism standards are only one part of the puzzle. In addition, teachers and teacher candidates must undergo anti-racism training. Only through these methods will white teachers, administrators, and teacher educators understand the depths to which they must reach to access the tools that they can use to support POC in their fight against white supremacy. Examples of appropriate curriculum and frameworks include the Anti-Defamation League (https://www.adl.org), which provides a variety of antibias training for students and teachers, The National Conference of Community and Justice of Metropolitan St. Louis (https://www.nccjstl.org/), and Crossroads Anti-RacismOrganizing and Training Chicago, IL (http://crossroadsantiracism.org/).

For white teachers at all levels working with students of color, we provide resources throughout this chapter as well as a reading list in Appendix I. While it is our intention to provide resources and recommendations that will assist teacher educators in this task that must be undertaken, we must also provide a warning—making change is not a matter of simply purchasing or reading these books in an attempt to resolve the issue of systemic inequity in our nation's policies and resulting commonplace practices. White teachers need to do the work by getting involved, being active, being aware, and engaged with the current issues of Black and Brown people, but first and foremost they need to do their own work and examine their own whiteness. White people need to talk to other white people about the work that must be done. We cannot stress strongly enough how unacceptable it is for a teacher to read this, or one of our recommended books, and to stop at that point. There is an ontology, a metacognition, an ongoing deep and meaningful reflection that needs to be begun among white educators, both about the privilege that a white teacher holds as a white citizen in the United States, and the cost of that privilege to people of color. White teachers need to recognize that by benefiting from these systems, they are exacerbating the problem. The first step is to understand the need for and purpose of socially just practices both in their lives and in their classroom, and to build an authentic and meaningful relationship with their students by teaching in a way that casts aside top-down learning and shifts to a community-based perspective that honors all voices.

In addition to the recommendations in the paragraph above, Teacher educators serve as a quality check—once they themselves have begun the practice of implementing socially just practices in their lives and in their professions, they must model this practice and explain their thinking and teaching practice to the teacher candidates they instruct. The hypocrisy of simulated tolerance, or "I believe *this*, but I teach *that*" must be recognized and called out, by teachers about their own thinking and by teachers about the thinking of their peers. Read, observe, learn, and examine their own belief systems. Throughout this chapter, we will provide resources and recommendations that will assist teacher educators in this task that must be undertaken. We caution the reader in this sense: When a beginning teacher or teacher educator initially models self-reflection (about their own teaching) in front of their students, there quite possibly will be a tendency for the teacher candidates to assume that their professor is unsure of themselves, and that is why they are demonstrating this type of thinking. Our white American masculine culture does not lend itself to public personal reflection. It is at times seen as weak, and teacher candidates, being at the beginning of their cognitive journey, may not understand this distinction and end up disregarding or discounting the instructor who is modeling this practice.

It is the role of the teacher educator and teacher education program to bridge theory and practice for their students, and it stands to reason that careful field placement experiences must be chosen. In areas where Black and Brown students are of a minimum number, placement officers, university supervisors, and program directors must be aware of the political and cultural views of the cooperating teacher with which the teacher candidate is placed. Teacher candidates of color entering all or mostly white schools can have a range of positive and negative experiences, as well as well-meaning but misintended negative experiences with students, faculty, and administrative professionals. In this case, the university representatives need to periodically check in with students of color, relying on the established supportive relationship they have cultivated with these students of color so that they feel safe addressing these issues with their university mentors. Placing teacher candidates of color with cooperating teachers of color is beneficial, as it provides support for the questions the teacher candidate may have, and many of these questions may have to do with how to stay mentally, emotionally, and spiritually healthy in a white supremacist society.

Teacher Educator Programs need to address their method of teaching classroom management. In virtually every classroom management course, behaviorism is the go-to for most teacher educators. When "sticking with what works" means relying on a model for classroom management that was first implemented in dogs at the turn of the century, something is clearly misaligned. The treatment of students with Black and Brown bodies in America's classrooms must be acknowledged by teacher educators, and they must cast aside antiquated belief systems and cease perpetuating these belief systems in their classroom management curriculum, texts, and instruction.

Preservice teachers of all races are proceeding through a cognitive growth as they learn how to teach, mentor, and support their students. A teacher education program is a time of great change. Teacher candidates seem to transform before our very eyes, but the person who returns at the end of student teaching bears no semblance to the neophyte who began student teaching yet four months prior. It is important to keep in mind that it is our role to foster the growth of this "still-adolescent," by supporting them with resources yet also challenging them to take initiative and use entrepreneurial skills they will need to rely on as an in-service teacher.

## RECOMMENDATIONS FOR PRESERVICE TEACHERS

At the time of publication, our preservice teachers fall into the socially constructed category of "Generation Z." The Pew Research Center confirms that individuals born after 1996 are more racially and ethnically diverse than any previous generation and, therefore, see the country's growing racial and ethnic diversity as a good thing. They are more likely to be the child of at least one immigrant parent, and they are also more likely to say that Blacks are treated less fairly than whites in this country (Parker and Igielnik, 2018). The fact that these preservice teachers are both more likely to have a college-educated parent than the previous generations, and their tendency to look to the government to solve problems, rather than businesses and individuals, creates new demand for teacher educators and systemic policies.

We encourage preservice teachers to start here, and to seek out books, podcasts, and videos that will provide them with information on how to "do the work" that is required to examine their implicit biases, white privilege, and complacency—not just because it is beneficial to the students they do and will teach, but because examining these traits is what will be needed to heal American communities, the country, the world, and the people who live within these borders. In a recent Education Week Teacher article, Joe Truss gives advice to white teachers in the areas of systemic racism and learning, interrupting racism in schools, relationships and classroom management, teaching and learning, and continual learning and reflection. "When you find yourself getting overwhelmed, feeling guilty, and wanting to burden a Brown person, stop. Find a few White folks to talk to about Whiteness and anti-Blackness. Read about White fragility and push through it. Push others through it and engage in White affinity anti-racist conversations" (Ferlazzo, 2020). The time for deep reflection is overdue. Epithets, palliative actions, and reassurances to oneself that "I'm not a racist" are no longer useful.

## RECOMMENDATIONS FOR IN-SERVICE PROFESSIONAL DEVELOPMENT ORGANIZERS

Professional educators must accept that society is unequal and based on socially constructed identities such as gender, race, sexuality, religious affiliation, social class, and other components of one's identity. Professional development for the in-service educator must start here. Explicitly teaching the Cycle of Socialization to educators supports them in learning how social identities are created and groups of individuals are privileged. Understanding the important roles that family, media, schools, and institutions play in this cycle can demonstrate how our biases are created and reinforced. Because most teachers are white females (USDE, 2016), they have been socialized to the myth of white supremacy and meritocracy in the United States. The mantra of these foundational ideas is that "we are all born on equal footing and our success or lack of success is due to personal work ethic and values." This ignores white supremacy and the institutional and systemic racism, sexism, classism at play within our society. Learning to take on a new perspective can take place in many forms. In-service educators can watch or attend lectures from academics that have studied and researched social justice issues, attend a professional book club reading and begin deconstructing these ideas, and/or watch documentaries addressing these topics (see resources in Appendix I). Joe Truss advises:

> Not every book is equal, especially for you. . . . When you've finished reading books written by white people for white people, read books written by Black people for white people, and finally, read books written by Black people for Black people. There's a difference. Notice the subtleties. You should be able to hear the message in all forms, but if you can't, explore why you can't. When you aren't emotionally triggered or playing devil's advocate, and your white

fragility isn't acting up as much as before, you will know you are making progress. (Ferlazzo, 2020)

The most powerful learning happens when people experience first hand what they are reading and/or discussing. Professional educators must experience marginalization and oppression in the forms of simulations. Allowing our majority white female teachers to experience an interaction with law enforcement as a Black male has a powerful impact that allows for the participant to feel oppression, some for the first time. Simulations of marginalization and oppression in a professional development workshop can have lasting impacts resulting in increased empathy and compassion for students with marginalized identities, an acknowledgment of social privilege, and a strong desire to create and maintain equitable access in the classroom (Adams and Bell, 2016).

Professional educators must be taught how to explicitly democratize their classroom space. In place of adhering to the tenets of behaviorism to control students within the classroom taught in virtually every classroom management course, in-service educators need to learn culturally responsive classroom management, trauma informed strategies, mental health supports, and removal of authoritarian practices. Honoring students' voices and empowering them in an inclusive classroom setting will result in a democratized space that allows our young students to participate in a democracy before coming to the age of maturity. Educators actively listening to students' stories without judgment, will reinforce their increased empathy and compassion previously learned. Creating the space for students to demonstrate their learning through a variety of assessments and providing opportunities for students to set their own pace for mastery of content are ways to ensure student voices are honored, and that top-down, authoritarian structures are removed from the classroom (Campano, 2007).

According to bell hooks, "making the classroom a democratic setting where everyone feels responsibility to contribute is a central goal of transformative pedagogy" (hooks p.39). Many teachers fear that classrooms will be uncontrollable and passions will ignite around the topics of racism, sexism, classism in the explicit teaching of these topics and, therefore, shy away from such topics in their teaching. As hooks states, there is a need to critically examine the way educators conceptualize the learning environment. One way to build community in a classroom and construct a democratized space is to honor every individual voice and note its value added to the class (hooks, 1994). It is most important to note that no one is ever an expert at first, but both educators and students must accept different ways of knowing and new epistemologies in an inclusive classroom.

Professional educators must strategically create an inclusive classroom community of learners with relationships that include traits of being accountable and demonstrating mutual respect. Mutual respect is the key to this community of learners. Removing the concept that the teacher is the keeper of all knowledge and students must learn and regurgitate the information is critical to building this fluid relationship (Ladson-Billings, 1995). Educators must also be active members of the community in which they teach, and when they are, they are able to reinforce this sense of community within the classroom. Developing an inclusive learning community requires representation of all identities, removal of heteronormativity, classism, patriarchy, and the Christian hegemony from our classroom spaces. Specific strategies to assist educators in minimizing or eliminating these from the classroom will need to be taught through professional development (Adams and Bell, 2016). Representation is key to the inclusivity of any space. Educators should ask themselves: Can your students see themselves in your decor, curricula, application of content examples, in the building? For example, for the early childhood teacher, are there only pictures of the heteronormative nuclear family in your unit of families? Where are the representations of homosexual families? Blended families? Step/multi-generational/foster families? Each type of family must be represented in your unit to include everyone in an equitable representation.

Professional development assists in-service educators to build a praxis of socially just curricula and culturally responsive instructional strategies, and these components are vital to democratizing classrooms and building learning communities. A praxis, or action plan, for teachers to introduce supplemental socially just curricula in combination with culturally responsive instructional strategies is vital in supporting in-service educators from removing the authoritarian structure in the classroom (figure 2.1). Professional development should focus on providing opportunities for each educator to construct their own praxis customized to the grade level and content discipline they are teaching. The praxis, defined by Paulo Freire, as the action and reflection of our practice. For educators, that means taking explicit action through instructional strategies to provide equitable access to high-quality education for all students. In addition, there must be continual personal reflection and awareness of our own implicit biases around marginalized identities (Freire, 1970).

This intense professional development is not available in a one-day workshop. Instead, a week of intense instruction on social justice, oppression and marginalization, implicit and explicit bias, and socialization is needed. Professional development should continue throughout the school year with facilitators and/or academic coaches working in classrooms with teachers until their instructional practices become second nature (Garmston and Wellman, 2009). Cognitive coaching, sustainable processes, in-place systems, transparency, and accountability are vital to supporting a paradigm shift within institutions.

## REQUIRED COMPONENTS TO CAUSE PARADIGM SHIFT FOR PUBLIC EDUCATION INSTITUTIONS, ADMINISTRATORS, AND STATE AGENCIES LEADING TO POLICY CHANGE

The first of these tenants is to understand that racism exists and is the foundation of our society (Delgado and Stefancic, 2001). Until public institutions admit that society is not merit based or inherently equal, they will never be able to understand the power dynamic at play in their own policies and practices. When socially constructed identities that are privileged and marginalized are ignored, institutions are permitted to be complicit in the power dynamics at play that create the inequity.

The second feature explains that racism is hard to eradicate because of the interest convergence of white elites and the white working class who benefit from the marginalization of Black and Brown folks (Delgado and Stefancic, 2001). This interest convergence is critical to the sustainability of the power dynamic to maintain one's own privilege. We see in chapter 3 that one of the main areas of little growth among preservice educators was that of academic standardized testing. According to Larke (1990), the lack of response (neutral answers in both the pre- and post-test condition) illustrates an unwillingness to state a true feeling, or a conflict of values. The authors purport that the preservice teachers surveyed actually know that these tests are not fair but are unwilling to admit this as this would potentially place their privilege in danger.

Social construction of identities and labels is the third feature of Critical Race Theory which is closely connected to the fourth feature of intersectionality of identities that create complexities in managing life (Delgado and Stefancic, 200). Explicit teaching of the Cycle of Socialization will support educators and institutions in understanding the source and benefit of the implicit and explicit bias they hold.

The final tenant of Critical Race Theory is honoring the voices of the marginalized. Voices of color hold credibility because of their expertise in the lived experience (Delgado and Stefancic, 2001). Active listening to the marginalized voices within the institution, strategic hiring of qualified professionals that hold marginalized identities, and the presence of people with marginalized identities in the hiring process and all decision-making bodies will support institutions as they move from a traditional model to a paradigm shift of equity and inclusion.

A full commitment to the four tenets of Critical Race Theory embedded in the mission and vision statements of the institution, as well as the explicit teaching of these tenants in the orientation of new hires will support the paradigm shift. Critical Race Theory is not enough. We must also tackle Whiteness and explicitly teach the construction of Whiteness in this country and the systems of privilege attached to it. Teaching the 600 years of Whiteness as a social construction in this country gives exposure to the institutionalization of racism and social inequity (dismantling racism, 2009). After gaining a complete understanding of the construction on Whiteness is mastered, the institutions must review their policies and practices for inherent Whiteness. The process of deconstructing the Whiteness and Eurocentrism embedded within their policies and practices at each level and department support these institutions in being able to dismantle their own white supremacy.

The proposed strategies and professional development for educators mentioned here are both a goal and a process. Teaching is a social enterprise laden with moral responsibility. As teacher-learners we explore the cultural diversity in our society, our schools, and in ourselves. As we come to a better knowledge of those forces that cause oppression to members of diverse cultures, we will begin to confront how those forces might be embedded in our own attitudes. As "teachers, learners and leaders," we must be willing to act as agents for social justice in our classrooms and schools. This requires the development of our own dispositions, cultural knowledge and competencies and resources to adopt curriculum and instructional skills for a culturally responsive classroom practice. Becoming more informed about the experiences of oppressed people ideally will lead to each educator's "praxis," a social consciousness combined with a plan for social action. When educators experience such "praxis" they become better prepared to be leaders in schools. Ultimately then, educators are to become enlightened about the experiences of people who are not members of the privileged "dominant hegemony" and what forces are operating in our classrooms to prevent social equality. As we deconstruct ways teachers, too, may inadvertently collude with the forces of oppression, we also examine practical ways to become facilitators of social change through education. As educators, we will be called to act as agents for social justice in our classrooms and in our schools.

# Appendix I

## Reading List for White Teachers of Brown Students

Loewen, James (1995), *Lies My Teacher Told Me: Everything Your American History Textbook Got Wrong*
Painter, Nell Irvin (2010), *The History of White People*
Alexander, Michelle (2010), *The New Jim Crow: Mass Incarceration in the Age of Colorblindness*
Smith, Chip (2007), *The Cost of Privilege: Taking on the System of White Supremacy and Racism*
Zinn, Howard (1980), *A People's History of the United States*
Wise, Tim (2008), *White Like Me: Reflections on Race from a Privileged Son*
Wise, Tim (2008), *Speaking Treason Fluently: Anti-Racist Reflections from an Angry White Male.*
Delpit, Lisa (1995), *Other People's Children: Cultural Conflict in the Classroom*
Wise, Tim (2010), *Colorblind: The Rise of Post Racial Politics and the Retreat from Racial Equity*
Harris-Lacewell, Melissa (2004), *Barbershops, Bibles, and BET: Everyday Talk and lack Political Thought.*
Wells, Amy Stuart and Robert L. Crain (1997), *Stepping Over the Colorline: African-American Students in White Suburban Schools*
Delpit, Lisa and Joanne Kilgour Dowdy, *The Skin That We Speak: Thoughts on Language and Culture in the Classroom.*
hooks, bell (1981), *Ain't I a Woman: Black Women and Feminism*
Tatum, Beverly Daniel (1997), *Why Are All the Black Kids Sitting Together in the Cafeteria? And Other Conversations about Race.*
LaRosa-Stern, Caryl and Ellen Hofheimer Bettmann (2000), *Anti-Defamation League's Hate Hurts: How Children Learn and Unlearn Prejudice*
Kozol, Jonathan (2005), *The Shame of the Nation: The restoration of Apartheid Schooling in America*
Wise, Tim (2009), *Between Barack and a Hard Place: Racism and White Denial in the Age of Obama*

Freire, Paulo (2011), *Pedagogy of the Oppressed*
hooks, bell (1995), *Killing Rage: Ending Racism*
Kitwana, Bakari (2002), *The Hip Hop Generation: Young Blacks and the Crisis in African-American Culture*
Bell, Derrick (1948), *Faces at the Bottom of the Well: The Permanence of Racism*
Lipsitz, George (2011), *How Racism Takes Place*
Brandt, Joseph (1991), *Dismantling Racism: The Continuing Challenge to White America*
Kivel, Paul (1995), *Uprooting Racism: How White People Can Work for Racial Justice*
Feinberg, Leslie (1996), *Transgender Warriors*
Berger, Maurice (1999), *White Lies: Race and the Myths of Whiteness*
DiAngelo, Robin (2018), *White Fragility: Why It's So Hard for White People to Talk About Racism*
Coates, Ta-Nehisi (2015), *Between the World and Me*
Ortiz, Paul (2018) *An African American and LatinX History of the United States*

# Appendix II
## *Sample of Course Description for Teacher Educators*

This course examines the social, economic, and political organization of public education in the United States, with a particular emphasis on the implications for historically marginalized populations. This course is required for all education students. The course explores diversity and multiculturalism on the individual as well as institutional level, with a focus on concepts such as privilege, discrimination, racism, and social transformation.

Teaching is a social enterprise laden with moral responsibility. This semester, as learners, we explore the cultural diversity in our society, our schools, and ourselves. As we come to a better knowledge of those forces which cause oppression to members of diverse cultures, we will begin to confront how those forces might be embedded in our own attitudes. As "teachers, learners and leaders," we must be willing to act as agents for social justice in our classrooms and schools. This course helps students acquire the dispositions, cultural knowledge, and competencies to adopt curriculum and instructional skills for a culturally responsive classroom practice. Becoming more informed about the experiences of oppressed people ideally will lead to each class member's "praxis," a social consciousness combined with a plan for social action. When future teachers experience such "praxis" they become better prepared to be leaders in schools. Ultimately the purpose of the course, then, is to become enlightened about the experiences of people who are not members of the privileged "dominant hegemony" and what forces are operating in our classrooms to prevent social equality. As we look at ways teachers, too, may be inadvertently colluding with the forces of oppression, we will examine practical ways to become facilitators of social change through education. Students will become thoroughly versed in multicultural education (ME) theory.

This course is designed to help students understand that teaching is essentially a social enterprise invested with moral responsibility and that, as teachers, they will be called to act as agents for social justice in their classrooms and in their schools. Through readings, activities, and class discussions, prospective teachers will examine attitudes and behaviors, which prevent classrooms, schools, and society from being fair and equitable for all students, and will commit to a personal plan of action for providing meaningful and equitable educational opportunities for all of their students. This course will help students acquire the dispositions, cultural knowledge, and competencies to adapt their curriculum and instructional skills for culturally responsive classroom practice.

# Bibliography

Adams, Maurienne and Lee Anne Bell, eds. 2016. *Teaching for Diversity and Social Justice*, 3rd Edition. New York: Routledge.

Allard, A.C. 2006. "A bit of a chameleon act: A case study of one teacher's understanding of diversity." *European Journal of Teacher Education* 29 (3): 319-340. https://doi.org/10.1080/02619760600795155.

Alexander, Kern and M. David. Alexander. 2009. *American Public School Law*, 7th Edition. California: Wadsworth Cengage Learning.

American Bar Association, *Resolution to House of Delegates*, 1 San Diego, CA (2001).

Anderson, Celia Rousseau and Beverly E. Cross. 2013. "What is "Urban? A CRT Examination of the Preparation of K-12 Teachers of Urban Schools." In *The Handbook of Critical Race Theory in Education*, edited by Marvin Lynn and Adrienne D. Dixon. 386-396. New York: Routledge.

Annamma, Subini Ancy. 2015. "Whiteness as property: Innocence and Ability in Teacher Education". *Urban Review* 47 (2): 293-316. https://doi.org/10.1007/s11256-014-0293-6.

Au, Wayne. 2014. "Decolonizing the Classroom: Lessons in Multicultural Education." In *Re-thinking Multicultural Education: Teaching for Racial and Cultural Justice*, 2nd Edition, edited by Wayne Au, 247-54. Wisconsin: Rethinking Schools, Ltd.

Banks, James A. 1993. "Multicultural Education: Historical Development, Dimensions, and Practice." *Review of Research in Education* 19: 3-49. https://www.jstor.org/stable/1167339?seq=1

Bauer, Natalee K. 2020. "What's Love Got to Do With It? Toward a Theory of Benevolent Whiteness in Education. *The Urban Review*. https:/doI.org/10.1007/s11256-020-00592-w

Bell, Leann. 2016. "Theoretical Foundations for Social Justice Education." In *Teaching for Diversity and Social Justice, 3rd Edition*, edited by Maurianne Adams, Lee Anne Bell, & Pat Griffin, 1-14. New York: Routledge.

Bell, Leann, Diane J. Goodman, and Mathew L. Ouellett. 2016. "Design and Facilitation." In *Teaching for Diversity and Social Justice, 3rd Edition*, edited by Maurianne Adams, Lee Anne Bell, & Pat Griffin. New York: Routledge.

Bigelow, Bill. 2014. "Standards and Tests Attack Multiculturalism." In *Rethinking Multicultural Education, 2nd Edition*. Wisconsin: Rethinking Schools, Ltd.

Bigelow, Bill. 2014. "Once Upon a Genocide: Columbus in Children's Literature." In *Re-thinking Multicultural Education: Teaching for Racial and Cultural Justice, 2nd Edition*, edited by Wayne Au. Wisconsin: Rethinking Schools, Ltd.

Bigelow, Bill. 2014. "Those Awful Texas Social Studies Standards: And What About Yours?" In *Re-thinking Multicultural Education: Teaching for Racial and Cultural Justice, 2nd Edition*, edited by Wayne Au. Wisconsin: Rethinking Schools, Ltd.

Bleakley, Paul & Cindy Bleakley. 2018. "School Resource Officers, 'Zero Tolerance Policies' and the Enforcement of Compliance in the American School System." *Interchange* 49: 247-261. https://doi.org/10.1007/s10780-018-9326-5.

Bohinski, Chesla Ann and Leventhal, Yumei. 2015. "Rethinking the ICC Framework: Transformation and Telecollaboration." *Foreign Language Annals* 48 (3): 521-534. https://doi.org/10.1111/flan.12149.

Brady, Kevin P. 2001. "Zero Tolerance or (In)Tolerance Policies--Weaponless School Violence, Due Process, and the Law of Student Suspensions and Expulsions: An Examination of Fuller v. Decatur Public School Board of Education School District." *B.Y.U. Education and Law Journal* 1 (7) 159-209. https://digitalcommons.law.byu.edu/elj/vol2002/iss1/7.

Breck, Susan E. and Jessica S. Krim. 2012. "Practice-based Teaching: A Self-study by Two Teacher Educators at the Graduate Level." *Studying Teacher Education* 8 (3): 289-302. https://doi.org/10.1080/17425964.2012.719126.

Breede, David, Tiffany Julian, David Langdon, George McKittrick, Beethika Khan, and Mark Doms. 2011. Executive Summary, Issue Brief #4-11, U.S. Department of Commerce- Economics and Statistics Administration. August, 2011. https://files.eric.ed.gov/fulltext/ED523766.pdf.

Brookfield, Stephen. (ed.). 2018. *Training Educators of Adults: The Theory and Practice of Graduate Adult Education*. Oxfordshire: Taylor & Francis.

Brookfield, Stephen. 1987. *Developing Critical Thinkers Challenging Adults to Explore Alternative Ways of Thinking and Acting*. San Francisco, CA: Jossey-Bass.

Brown, Elinor. 2004. "What Precipitates Change in Cultural Diversity Awareness during a Multicultural Course: The Message or the Method?" *Journal of Teacher Education* 55 (4): 325-340. https://doi.org/10.1177/0022487104266746.

Bryan, Nathaniel. 2017. "White Teachers' Role in Sustaining the School-to-Prison Pipeline: Recommendations for Teacher Education". *Urban Review* 45 (3): 326-345. https://doi.org/10.1007/s11256-017-0403-3.

Burbach, Barbara and Thurman D. Nassoiy. 2004. "Where Is Equity in the National Standards? A Critical Review of the INTASC, NCATE, and NBPTS Standards." *Journal for Scholar-Practitioner Learner*. 2 (4) 29-43.

Burbules, Nicholas. 1997. "A grammar of difference: some ways of re-thinking difference and diversity as educational topics." *Australian Educational Researcher* 24 (1): 97-116. ttps://doi.org/10.1007/BF03219643.

Burris, Carol Corbett and Delia T. Garrity. 2008. *Detracking for Excellence and Equity*. Virginia: Association for Supervision and Curriculum Development.

Campano, George. 2007. "Honoring Student Stories." *Educational Leadership* 65 (2): 48-54.

Carberry, Devin. 2014. "Precious Knowledge: Teaching Solidarity with Tucson." In *Re-thinking Multicultural Education: Teaching for Racial and Cultural Justice, 2nd Edition*, edited by Wayne Au. Wisconsin: Rethinking Schools, Ltd.

Casella, Ronnie. 2003. "Zero Tolerance Policy in Schools: Rationale, Consequences, and Alternatives". *Teachers College Record* 105 (5): 872-92. https://doi.org/10.1111/1467-9620.00271.

Chapman, Thankdeka K. 2013. "Origins of and Connections to Social Justice in Critical Race Theory in Education." In *The Handbook of Critical Race Theory in Education*, edited by Marvin Lynn and Adrienne D. Dixon. 101-111. New York: Routledge.

Cilluffo, A. and Cohn, D. 2017. "10 Demographic Trends Shaping the U.S. and the World in 2017." Pew Research Center. 2017. Accessed August 30, 2020. http://www.pewresearch.org/fact-tank/2017/04/27/10-demographic-trends-shaping-the-u-s-and-the-world-in-2017/.

Cornbleth C. and Dexter Waugh. 1995. *The great speckled bird: Multicultural Politics and Education*. New York: Routledge.

Crenshaw, Kimberle. 1989. "Demarginalizing the Intersection of Race and Sex: A Black Feminist Critique of Antidiscrimination Doctrine, Feminist Theory and Antiracist Politics." *University of Chicago Legal Forum*: Vol. 1989, Article 8. Accessed August 30, 2020. https://chicagounbound.uchicago.edu/uclf/vol1989/iss1/8.

Delgado, Richard and Jean Stefancic. 2001. *Critical Race Theory: An Introduction*. New York and London: New York University Press.

Delpit, Lisa, 1996. *Other People's Children: Conflict in the Classroom*. New York: New Press.

Diamond, Barbara J. and Margaret A. Moore. 1995. *Multicultural Literacy; Mirroring the Reality of the Classroom*. New York: Longman Publishers.

DiAngleo, Robin. 2018. *White Fragility: Why it's so Hard for White People to Talk About Racism*. Massachusetts: Beacon Press.

Dismantling Racism. 2009. "History of the Race Construct." History Script. Accessed August 30, 2020. www.dismantlingracism.org.

Dumas, Michael J. 2015. "Against the Dark: Antiblackness in Education Policy and Discourse." *Theory into Practice* 55 (1): 11-19. https://doi.org/10.1080/00405841.2016.1116852.

Dumas, Michael J. & Kihana Miraya Ross. 2016. "Be Real Black for Me: Imagining BlackCrit in Education." *Urban Education* 51 (4): 415-442. https://doi.org/10.1177/0042085916628611.

*edglossary*, s.v. "multicultural education." Accessed March 6, 2016, https://www.edglossary.org/multicultural-education/.

Eppley, Karen, Patrick Shannon, and Lauren K. Gilbert. 2011. "Did you like living in a trailer? Why or why not?: Discourse and the third space in a rural pen pal exchange." *Teaching and Teacher Education* 27 (2): 289–297. https://doi.org/10.1016/j.tate.2010.08.011.

Evans-Winters, Venus and Pamela Twyman Hoff. 2011. "The aesthetics of White racism in pre-service teacher education: a critical race theory perspective." *Race Ethnicity and Education*, 14 (4): 461-479. https://doi.org/10.1080/13613324.2010.548376.

Ferlazzo, Larry. 2020. "Advice for the Newly Woke White Teachers on Teaching Black Children." *Education Week Teacher*. June 3, 2020. Accessed August 30, 2020. https://blogs.edweek.org/teachers/classroom_qa_with_larry_ferlazzo/2020/06/advice_for_the_newly_woke_white_teachers_on_teaching_black_children.html.

Ford, James E. 2016. "The Root of Discipline Disparity." *Educational Leadership* 72 (3): 42-46.

Furtado, K., Duncan, A., Kocher, J., Nandan, P. 2019. *Falling Through the Cracks: Disparities in Out of School Suspension in St. Louis at the Intersection of Race, Disability, and Gender.* Retrieved from www.forwardthroughferguson.org.

Foucault, Michel. 1991. "Governmentality." In *The Foucault Effect. Studies of Governmentality,* edited by Graham Burchell, Colin Gordon, and Peter Miller. 88-104. Chicago: University of Chicago Press.

Freire, Paulo, 1970. *Pedagogy of the Oppressed.* New York: Bloomsbury Publishing.

Freis, Kim and Todd A. DeMitchell. 2007. "Zero Tolerance and the Paradox of Fairness: Viewpoints from the Classroom." *Journal of Law and Education* 36 (2): 211-229. https://doi.org/10.1080/00131946.2015.1120205.

Garnston, Robert J. and Bruce Wellman. 2009. *The Adaptive School: A Sourcebook for Developing Collaborative Groups.* Maryland: Christopher- Gordon Publication.

Gay, Geneva. 2010. *Culturally Responsive Teaching Theory, Research, and Practice, 2nd Edition.* New York: Teachers College Press.

Gersman, Elinor Mondale. 1972. "The Development of Public Education for Blacks in Nineteenth Century St. Louis, Missouri". *The Journal of Negro Education* 41 (1): 35-47. https://www.jstor.org/stable/2967029.

Grant, Nigel. 1997. "Some Problems of Identity and Education: A Comparative Examination of Multicultural Education." *Comparative Education* 33 (1): 9-28. https://doi.org/10.1080/03050069728613.

Gillborn, David. 2005. "Educational Policy as an Act of White Supremacy: Whiteness, Critical Race Theory, and Educational Reform." *Journal of Educational Policy* 20 (4): 485-505. https://doi.org/10.1080/02680930500132346.

Gillborn, David. 2013. "The Policy of Inequity: Using CRT to Unmask White Supremacy in Education Policy." In *The Handbook of Critical Race Theory in Education,* edited by Marvin Lynn and Adrienne D. Dixon. New York: Routledge.

Gorski, Paul C. and Seema G. Pothinin. 2014. *Case Studies on Diversity and Social Justice Education.* New York: Routledge.

Gupta, Akhil and James Ferguson. 1997. *Culture Power Place: Explorations in Critical Theory.* Durham and London: Duke University Press.

Haley, Marjorie Hall. 2012. "An Online Cultural Exchange in Pre-service Language Teacher Education: A Dialogic Approach to Understanding." *US-China Education Review* B (5): 528-533.

Harris, Brenda G., Hayes, Cleveland, and Smith, Darron T. 2019. "Not a 'Who Done It Mystery:' On How Whiteness Sabotages Equity Aims in Teacher Preparation Programs. *The Urban Review*. 52: 198-213.

Henry, Gertrude B. 1986. *Cultural diversity awareness inventory*. Virginia: Hampton University Mainstreaming Outreach Project. (ERIC Document Reproduction Service No. ED282657).

hooks, bell. 1994. *Teaching to Transgress: Education as the Practice of Freedom*. New York: Tyler and Francis Group.

hooks, bell. 1984. *Feminist Theory From Margin to Center*. Boston: South End Press

Howard, Gary R. 2006. *We can't teach what we don't know: White teachers, multiracial schools*. New York: Teachers College Press.

Howard, Tyrone. 2010. *Why Race and Culture Matter in Schools: Closing the Achievement Gap in America's Classrooms* (Multicultural Education Series). New York: Teachers College Press.

Hispanic Association of Colleges and Universities. 2020. "Hispanic Association of Colleges and Universities (HACU) Map of HSIs and e-HSIs: 2016-2017." Accessed May 25, 2020. https://hacuadvocates.net/hacu/HSImap#5/48.035/-96.863.

The HBCU Library Alliance. 2020. "The HBCU Library Alliance: An Overview." Accessed May 25, 2020. https://slideplayer.com/slide/10964601/.

Jaschik, Scott. 2020. New Evidence of Racial Bias on SAT." Inside Higher Ed website. Accessed August 30, 2020. https://www.insidehighered.com/news/2010/06/21/new-evidence-racial-bias-sat.

Kessen, William. 2005. "The American Child and Other Cultural Inventions." In *The Critical Middle School Reader*, edited by Enora Brown and Kenneth Saltman. 57-64. New York: Routledge.

Krim, Jessica S., Laleh E. Coté, Renée S. Schwartz, Elisa M. Stone, Jessica J. Cleeves, Kelly J. Barry, Wilella Burgess, et al. "Models and Impacts of Science Research Experiences: A Review of the Literature of CUREs, UREs, and TREs." *CBE—Life Sciences Education* 18 (44): 1-14. https://doi.org/10.1187/cbe.19-03-0069.

Ladson-Billings, Gloria. 2009. "Just What is Critical Race Theory and What's it Doing in a Nice Field Like Education?" In *Foundations of Critical Race Theory in Education*, edited by; Edward Taylor, David Gillborn. and Gloria Ladson-Billings. New York: Routledge.

Ladson-Billings, Gloria. 2010. "New Directions in Multicultural Education Complexities, Boundaries, and Critical Race Theory. In *The Handbook of Research on Multicultural Education*. New York: Routledge.

Ladson Billings, Gloria and William F. Tate. 1995. "Towards a Critical Race Theory of Education." In *Critical Race Theory in Education: All God's Children Got a Song*, edited by Adrienne D. Dixson, Celia K. Rousseau Anderson, Jamel K. Donnor. New York: Routledge.

Ladson-Billings, Gloria. 1995. "Toward a Theory of Culturally Relevant Pedagogy." *American Educational Research Journal* 32 (3): 465- 491. https://doi.org/10.3102/00028312032003465.

Lapayese, Yvette V., Aldana, Ursula S., and Lara, Eduardo. 2014. "A Racio-economic Analysis of Teach For America: Counterstories of TFA Teachers of Color." *Perspectives on Urban education* 11 (1): 11-25.

Larke, Patricia. 1990. "Cultural Diversity Awareness Inventory: Assessing the Sensitivity of Preservice Teachers." *Action in Teacher Education* 12 (3): 23-30. https://doi.org/10.1080/01626620.1990.10734396.

Larotta, Clarena. and Arlene F. Serrano. 2012. "Pen Pal Writing: A Holistic and Socio-Cultural Approach to Adult English Literacy." *Journal of Adult Education* 1 (41): 8-18.

Lawrence, Richard. 2007. *School Crime and Juvenile Justice*. New York: Oxford University Press.

Liaw, Meei-Ling. 1998. "Using electronic mail for English as a Foreign Language instruction." *System* 26 (3): 335-351. https://doi.org/10.1016/S0346-251X(98)00025-6.

Loewenberg Ball, D., and Francesca M. Forzani. 2009. "The Work of Teaching and the Challenge for Teacher Education." *Journal of Teacher Education* 60 (5): 497–511. https://doi.org/10.1177/0022487109348479/.

Lortie, Dan. 1975. *Schoolteacher: A sociological study.* Illinois: University of Chicago Press.

Marshall, Jennifer. 2014. *Introduction to Comparative and International Education.* California: SAGE.

Matias, Cheryl E., Allison Henry, & Craig Darland. 2017. "The Twin Tales of Whiteness: Exploring the Emotional Rollercoaster of Teaching and Learning about Whiteness." *Taboo: The Journal of Culture and Education*, 16 (1): 7-29. https://doi.org/10.31390/taboo.16.1.04.

Matias, Cheryl E., Roberto Montoya, and Naomi W.I. Nishi. 2016. "Blocking CRT: How the Emotionality of Whiteness Blocks CRT in Urban Teacher Education". *Educational Studies* 52 (1): 1-19. https://doi.org/10.1080/00131946.2015.1120205.

Matias, Cheryl E., Kara Mitchell Viesca, Dorothy F. Garrison-Wade, Madhavi Tandon & Rene Galindo. 2014. "What is Critical Whiteness Doing in OUR Nice Field like Critical Race Theory?: Applying CRT and CWS to Understand the White Imaginations of White Teacher Candidates." *Equity & Excellence in Education* 47(3): 289-304. https://doi.org/10.1080/10665684.2014.933692.

McGee, Ebony and Lydia Bentley. 2017. "The Equity Ethic: Black and LatinX College Students Reengineering their STEM Careers towards Justice." *American Journal of Education* 124 (1): 1-36. https://doi.org/10.1086/693954.

McMillon, Gwendolyn Michele Thompson. 2009. "Pen Pals Without Borders: A Cultural Exchange of Teaching and Learning." *Education and Urban Society,* 42 (1): 119-135. https://doi.org/10.1177/0013124509336066.

McNiff, Jean. 2013. *Action Research: Principles and Practice, 3rd Edition.* New York: Routledge.

Mezirow, Jack. 1997. "Transformative Learning: Theory to Practice." *New Directions for Adult and Continuing Education* 74: 5-12. https://doi.org/10.1002/ace.7401.

Milner, Richard H. IV, F. Alvin Pearman III, and Ebony O. McGhee. 2013. "Critical Race Theory, Interest Convergence, and Teacher Education." In *The Handbook of Critical Race Theory in Education,* edited by Marvin Lynn and Adrienne D. Dixon. 339-354. New York: Routledge.

Multicultural Education. 2020. "Glossary of Education Reform." Accessed August 30, 2020. https://www.edglossary.org.

National Center for Educational Statistics. 2015. "Nation's Report Card." Accessed April 1, 2020. https://nces.ed.gov/nationsreportcard/studies/gaps/.

NEA Today Online. n.d. "Multicultural Education Dimensions and Paradigms." Accessed August 30, 2020. https://learner.org/wp-content/uploads/2019/02/3.Multiculturalism.pdf.

Ngo, Bic. 2010. "Doing Diversity at Dynamic High: Problems and Possibilities of Multicultural Education in Practice." *Education and Urban Society* 42 (4): 473-495. https://doi.org/10.1177/0013124509356648.

Nieto, S. 2010. *The Light in Their Eyes: Creating Multicultural Communities* (10th anniversary ed.). New York: Teachers College Press.

Oluo, Ijeoma. 2019. *So You Want to Talk about Race.* New York: Seal Press.

Partnership for 21st Century Learning. 2019. "Framework for 21st Century Learning." Accessed March 6, 2016. http://static.battelleforkids.org/documents/p21/P21_Framework_Brief.pdf.

Peguero, Anthony A., Jennifer M. Bondy, and Zahra Shekarhar. 2017. "Punishing Latina/o Youth: School Justice, Fairness, Order, Dropping out, and Gender Disparities". *Hispanic Journal of Behavioral Sciences* 39 (1): 98-125. https://doi.org/10.1177/0739986316679633.

Parker, Kim and Ruth Igielnik. 2020. "On the Cusp of Adulthood and Facing an Uncertain Future: What We Know About Gen Z So Far." Pew Research Center, Social and Demographic Trends. Accessed August 30, 2020. https://www.pewsocialtrends.org/essay/on-the-cusp-of-adulthood-and-facing-an-uncertain-future-what-we-know-about-gen-z-so-far/.

Rabaka, Reiland. 2007. "The Souls of White Folk: W.E. B. DuBois's Critique of White Supremacy and Contributions of Critical White Studies." *Journal of African American Studies* 11 (1): 1-15. https://doi.org/10.1007/s12111-007-9011-8.

Ravitch, Diane. 2010. *The Death and Life of the Great American School System: How Testing and Choice are Undermining Education.* New York: Basic Books, PBG Publishing, LLC.

Richard, Jill. 2004. "Zero Room for Zero Tolerance: Rethinking Federal Funding for Zero Tolerance Policies". *University of Dayton Law Review* 30 (1): 91-117.

Rosales, John. 2018. "The Racist Beginnings of Standardized Testing: From grade school to college, students of color have suffered the effects of Biased testing." National Educators Association. Accessed June 10, 2020. http://www.nea.org/home/73288.htm.

Ryan, J., Antonis Katsiyannis, PhD, Jennifer M. Counts, MA, & Jil C Shelnut, MEd. 2017. "The Growing Concerns Regarding School Resource Officers." *Intervention in School and Clinic* 53 (3): 188-192. https://doi.org/10.1177/1053451217702108.

Saltman, Kenneth. 2005. "The Social Construction of Adolescence." In *The Critical Middle School Reader*, edited by Enora Brown and Kenneth Saltman, 15-20. New York: Routledge.

Samuels, Dena. 2014. *The Culturally Inclusive Educator: Preparing for a Multicultural World*. New York: Teachers College Press.

Shandomo, Hibajene M. 2009. "Getting to Knew You: Cross-Cultural Pen Pals Expand Children's World View." *Childhood Education* 85 (3): 154-159. https://doi.org/10.1080/00094056.2009.10521381.

Sleeter, Christian E. 2017. "Critical Race Theory and the Whiteness of Teacher Education." *Urban Education,* 52 (2): 155-169. https://doi.org/10.1177/0042085916668957.

Solorzano, Daniel G and Yosso, Tara J. 2002. "Critical Race Methodology: Counter Storytelling as an Analytical Framework for Educational Research." In *Foundations of Critical Race Theory in Education*, edited by Edward Taylor, David Gillborn. and Gloria Ladson-Billings. New York: Routledge.

Southern Poverty Law Center, Special Report. 2016. *The Trump Effect: The Impact of the 2016 Presidential Election on our Nation's Schools*. Retrieved from: https://www.tolerance.org/sites/default/files/2017-06/After%20the%20Election%20Trump%20Effect%20Report.pdf.

Spring, Joel H. 2018. *American Education*. New York: Routledge.

Tatum, Beverly Daniel. 1992. "Talking About Race, Learning About Racism: The Application of Racial Identity Development Theory in the Classroom.*" Harvard Educational Review*, 62 (1): 1-25.

Tatum, Beverly Daniel. 2009. "Teaching White Students About Racism: The Search for White Allies and the Restoration of Hope." In *Foundations of Critical Race Theory in Education*, edited by Edward Taylor, David Gillborn. and Gloria Ladson-Billings. New York: Routledge.

Troen, Selwyn K. 1973. "Popular Education in Nineteenth Century St. Louis." *History of Education Quarterly* 13 (1): 23-40. https://www.jstor.org/stable/366962.

United States Department of Education - National Council for Education Statistics (NCES). 2018. The Condition of Education 2018 (Report No. 2018-144). Retrieved from https://files.eric.ed.gov/fulltext/ED583502.pdf.

United States Department of Education. 2016. The State of Racial Diversity in the Educator Workforce. Office of Planning, Evaluation and Policy Development. Retrieved from https://www2.ed.gov/rschstat/eval/highered/racial-diversity/state-racial-diversity-workforce.pdf

Vespa, J., Armstrong, D.M., and Medina, L. 2018. Demographic Turning Points for the United States: Population Projections, for 2020-2060, P25-1144, United States Census Bureau, United States Department of Commerce, Economics and Statistics Administration. https://www.census.gov/content/dam/Census/library/publications/2018/demo/P25_1144.pdf.

Waddell, Jennifer H. 2013. "Working with Families in Urban Teacher Education: A Critical Need for All Students" *The Teacher Educator* 48 (4): 276-295. https://doi.org/10.1080/08878730.2013.826767.

Walker-Dalhouse, Doris and Dalhouse, A. Derrick. 2006. "Investigating white teacher candidates' beliefs about teaching in culturally diverse classrooms." *Negro Educational Review* 57 (1-2): 69-84.

Watson, Dyan, Jesse Habopian, & Wayne Au. 2018. *Teaching for Black Lives*, edited by Ari Bloomekatz. Milwaukee: Rethinking Schools Ltd.

White, Terrenda C. "Teach For America's Paradoxical Diversity Initiative: Race, Policy, and Black Teacher Displacement in Urban Schools." *Education Policy Analysis Archives* 24 (2016): 16. http://dx.doi.org/10.14507/epaa.24.2100.

Wilfong, Lori G. and Casey Oberhauser. 2012. "A Pen Pal Project Connects Teacher Candidates and Urban Youth" *Middle School Journal* 43 (5): 40-50. https://doi.org/10.1080/00940771.2012.11461828.

Willis, Arlette. Ingram, and Shuaib J. Meacham. 1996. "Break point: The challenges of teaching multicultural education courses." *The Journal of the Assembly for Expanded Perspectives on Learning* 2 (1): 8.

Wlodkowski, Raymond J. and Margery B. Ginsberg. 1995. "A Framework for Culturally Responsive Teaching." *Educational Leadership* 53 (1): 17-21.

Zinn, Howard. 1980. *A People's History of the United States*. New York: Harper Collins. 117 ALR 5th 459 (2004)

# Index

21st Century Learning, 14

ally, 21, 27, 95
anti-racism, 72–73, 95
assessment, viii, 1, 17, 19, 24, 41, 46–47, 50, 55–57, 65, 72, 77

Black Indigenous People of Color (BIPOC), 24
Brown *vs.* Board, 8, 62

Christian, 2, 30, 42, 46, 62, 66, 78, 92
colonization, 29, 30, 32–33, 69
columbine, 10
Critical Race Theory, 18, 27, 29, 30, 34–35, 59, 61, 63, 65, 67, 69, 79
Cultural Diversity Awareness Inventory (CDAI), 17, 43, 44, 46–50, 52, 54, 55, 57
culturally responsive pedagogy, 42, 48, 65–66, 71, 72, 77, 78, 80

demographics, 1–3, 6, 17, 41–43, 54, 63–64
discipline, 7, 10–12, 42, 59, 62–63, 68–69, 78, 88
disproportionality, 19, 21, 38

the equity group, 15
Eurocentric, 9, 19, 23, 25–26, 33–34, 60, 69–70

global demographic shift, 17

Hispanic Serving Institutions (HSI), 4
Historically Black Colleges and Universities (HBCU), 5–6
honoring, 15, 30, 77, 79

Indigenous, 6, 20, 24, 29, 32, 69
intersectionality, 19, 21, 30, 60–61, 79

LatinX, 6, 17, 24
laws, 7, 10, 20, 29, 31

marginalization, 16, 19–21, 23, 26, 29, 35–36, 39, 77–79
marginalized identities, 17, 20, 23, 25, 27, 30–31, 59, 62, 68–70, 77–79
microaggressions, 12, 21
migration, 1, 28, 30, 38
multicultural education, 13–14, 17, 19–25, 27, 29–34, 38–39, 42, 44, 47–48, 60, 83, 85–89, 91–93, 95

preservice teacher, 64
presidential administration, 15, 17
Primarily White Institutions (PWI), 6

racial composition of students, 2
racial inequity, 3, 66
racism, 26–27, 29, 31–33, 35–36, 38, 59, 61–63, 68, 69, 71, 76–77, 79, 80
Ruby Bridges, 8

sanctuary city, 15
School Resource Officer (SRO), 11
simulated tolerance, 13–14, 19, 41–42, 54–55, 58, 74
social justice education, 32, 34, 36, 38–39
St. Louis, 8, 73
stories (and histories), 9, 13, 22, 24, 34–35, 42, 61, 77
suspension, 3, 12

teacher candidates, 10, 13, 15, 17, 25–28, 30–31, 35–36, 38, 39, 41–45, 47, 52, 54–55, 60, 63, 66, 69, 72–75, 90, 93, 96, 98
teacher preparation program, vii, 3–6, 9, 13, 15–18, 22, 25–28, 33–34, 37, 39, 43, 60, 63–64, 66, 67–68, 72, 89, 96

Whiteness, 8–10, 15, 24, 27, 58, 60, 61, 63–66, 69, 73, 76, 79, 80
white privilege, 27, 61, 68, 75
white savior, 8
white spaces, 61
white supremacist, 6, 9, 16–18, 26–27, 30–31, 34, 61–63, 69, 75
white supremacist curriculum, 10, 13–15, 66
white supremacy, 9, 10, 16, 24–27, 32–33, 61–66, 68, 72–73, 76, 80

Zero Tolerance Policy (ZTP), 10–11

# About the Authors

Raised in Wilmington, Delaware, **Dr. Jessica S. Krim** began her career as a middle and high school science educator. With teaching experience on the Hopi Indian Reservation in Keams Canyon, Arizona, and Wilmington, Delaware, her experience as a teacher in these areas exposed her to inequities in both the Native American and African American population. Looking to make more of a difference in classrooms, she then obtained her Master's in Physical Science and Doctorate in Curriculum and Instruction. Dr. Krim's research centers around science education and critical reflection, especially as it pertains to equity, as is reflected in her publication *Models and Impacts of Science Research Experiences: A Review of the Literature of CUREs, UREs, and TREs*. She also studies how providing high-leverage practices for preservice teachers can impact their knowledge, skills, and dispositions and is currently conducting research in the cultural awareness of preservice teachers. One of her most recent initiatives is to implement a redesigned Secondary Education program that focuses on Critical Race Theory, Social Justice, and Anti-Racism. In addition to being a member of the DREAM Collective, she also serves as an associate professor, chair, and Secondary Education Program Director at Southern Illinois University at Edwardsville.

**Dr. Jennifer M. Hernandez** is a veteran special education teacher of fifteen years. She has primarily taught students with emotional disturbance, mental illness, and incarcerated youth in secondary alternative settings. In the last three years of her tenure in special education, Dr. Hernandez was a Special Education Administrator in the Ferguson-Florissant School District in Ferguson, MO. She was a witness and student advocate in the aftermath of the murder of Michael Brown and the community in trauma. She worked as an ally as the community responded with activism and the creation of Black

Lives Matter. Dr. Hernandez completed her PhD in 2013 from the University of Missouri-St. Louis in Educational Leadership and Policy Studies with a minor in social justice. The crux of her doctoral research included the critical analysis of racialized policies that facilitate the school-to-prison nexus. Dr. Hernandez began teaching pre-candidate teachers as an assistant professor in the School of Education at Quinnipiac University. She is currently teaching at Southern Illinois University in Edwardsville, IL, in the Secondary Program for Teaching and Learning. Dr. Hernandez focuses on anti-bias/anti-racism training for in-service educators and teacher candidates to address racism and all forms of oppression in public education.

www.ingramcontent.com/pod-product-compliance
Lightning Source LLC
Chambersburg PA
CBHW061720300426
44115CB00014B/2770